faith in real life

faith in real life

Creating Community in the Park, Coffee Shop, and Living Room

MIKE TATLOCK

ZONDERVAN®

ZONDERVAN.com/
AUTHORTRACKER
follow your favorite authors

ZONDERVAN

Faith in Real Life
Copyright © 2010 by Michael Tatlock

This title is also available as a Zondervan ebook.
Visit www.zondervan.com/ebooks.

This title is also available in a Zondervan audio edition.
Visit www.zondervan.fm.

Requests for information should be addressed to:
Zondervan, *Grand Rapids, Michigan 49530*

Library of Congress Cataloging-in-Publication Data

Tatlock, Mike, 1974.
      Faith in real life : creating community in the park, coffee shop, and living room /
Mike Tatlock.
            p.   cm.
      Includes bibliographical references.
      ISBN 978-0-310-29190-9 (softcover)
      1. Communities—Religious aspects—Christianity. 2. Fellowship—Religious
aspects—Christianity. I. Title.
BV4517.5T38   2010
261—dc22   2009010831

All Scripture quotations, unless otherwise indicated, are taken from the *Holy Bible,
Today's New International Version*™. TNIV®. Copyright © 2001, 2005 by Biblica, Inc. Used
by permission of Zondervan. All rights reserved.

Scripture quotations marked MSG are taken from *The Message.* Copyright © 1993, 1994,
1995, 1996, 2000, 2001, 2002. Used by permission of NavPress Publishing Group.

Cover illustration: iStockphoto®
Interior design: Beth Shagene

Printed in the United States of America

10 11 12 13 14 15 /DCI/ 23 22 21 20 19 18 17 16 15 14 13 12 11 10 9 8 7 6 5 4 3 2

To
my soul mate and wife, Bernadette—
your life portrays the essence of our Savior.
May we continue to risk all that we have
in order to be all that he wants us to be.

To
my family, who breathes life into me.
May we continue to live life
beyond normal ... to radical.

To
my community of friends,
who humble me as their shepherd.
May every moment we share
be a collision with the kingdom.

contents

Part 3

the coffee shop

Part 4

the living room

holy profanity

I have to confess—there was a time when my anger toward the church festered like a rancid wound. I had become a closet church hater. Early in my adult years I had turned my back on organized Christianity. The mere mention of the word *church* invoked a nightmare of wounded devastation. Those hurtful explosive words spoken by my fellow heaven-bounds suffocated the only breath of spiritual air I was breathing. Honestly, I would rather hang out with my cursing heathen friends. For some reason I didn't find their swearing quite as offensive in comparison to the hypocritical profanity spewed within the holy huddles of my Christian community. It seemed to me that uncensored arguments centered on carpet color, music selection, Bible translations, and self-preservation contributed more to the sacrilegious mockery of what it means to be God's people. A sort of spiritual Tourette's syndrome. I often felt that our off-the-cuff claims to be "Christian" might, in fact, be more vulgar and irreverent to our heavenly Savior than the fetid remarks of those who are not Christ-followers. There is nothing more profane than a lifestyle that haphazardly contradicts its confessions of faith. Even as I write this statement I am reminiscing over the words of the apostle John in 1 John 1:6: "If we claim to have fellowship with [God] yet walk in the darkness, we lie and do not live out the truth." An admonishing reminder that when our lives display inconsistency with our professed values, our tongues become a source of pious propaganda.

Drawing these conclusions led me to lose hope in what the church could be. Looking within the muted mirror of my soul exposed something far more disgusting and loathsome. It was my prideful, condescending attitude toward the church. I had come to expect perfection, when only Jesus Christ himself is entitled to claim flawlessness. With every criticism and disapproval of the church I dished out, my manner became more coarse and juvenile, revealing another kind of abrasive foul mouth. Every fault-finding commentary that I articulated only added to my own appalling utterance of profanity.

Deep down, I believe that authentic Christians want a faith that is more than just lip service to God and the world. We want to reconcile our faith with the realities of our daily lives. It's about our faith in real life, and it calls for an audacious optimism—an ability to see the bride of Christ the way the Bridegroom sees her. Faith in real life captures the optimism of what it means to be the church—as in *the community of God's people*. The church is a vibrant group of Christians expressing themselves through a community of faith that engages with the surrounding culture. Biblical community was designed to be a catalyst, moving people toward maximum impact and life-changing transformation. It is the vehicle to carry a vision forward by creating an infrastructure of relational influence. It is the soil in which organic ministry opportunities and leaders grow. It values church as more of a process than an event. It defines success not by numbers, buildings, or programs but by life change. Biblical community merges our faith into real life.

This kind of movement begins when a church develops a clear, intentional strategy to connect people and provoke them to be about something bigger than themselves. Momentum is generated in a culture where people long to be part of a cause more than being part of a congregation, thus creating a network of lives bonded together through authentic relationships.

I guess you could call me a recovering church hater. (Emphasis on *recovering*. Even my first draft of this book still had undertones that came across as negative. Hey, I'm healing.) The Bible uses the word *holy* to mean "sacred" or "set apart for a special purpose." A holy life is about living to the fullness of what life was "set apart" for in the first place. Anything else is profane.

I'm writing this book because I love the church and can envision all that it could be. This book reflects my own journey toward a new way of thinking about how church is done. It gives an account of failures that fueled new ideas. I'm not trying to supply a model, but tell a story of how we have structured our church to connect, empower, and release people with passion. The idea is to cultivate a deeper understanding of the shift that needs to take place if churches want to implement a simplified strategy of ministry that connects faith with real life.

This book examines the life of Jesus in relation to his desire to see others invited into community. Jesus loved to see messy lives intersect and become beacons for the gospel. Many churches want to experience true biblical community. My ambition is to stimulate people to prioritize and embrace the outrageous intent of community in their churches.

Part 1

the new church

1

the church and the chihuahua club

Becoming a Church Leader

"I never want to be a pastor!" Those were words that repeatedly echoed in my heart growing up. It's almost cliché to say that I, who now love my career choice, once considered church leadership to be the dirtiest job ever. I believed that being a pastor was the equivalent of having a root canal without Novocain—a self-induced decision that would inflict pain to the roots of my soul. It seemed so masochistic.

Having grown up as a pastor's kid, I was all too familiar with the exhaustive conversations that centered on church and church issues. Whether it was in the car (we were a family of six that crammed into a 1973 Gremlin) or around the dinner table, we were always discussing the subculture of Christians and their gathering place called *church*.

Those who were unchurched were a recurring topic of conversation. It wasn't unchurched people whom we spent hours talking about; it was church people and their intolerant response to the unchurched. My father had a passion to reach those outside the church and love them into a growing relationship with their Redeemer. He also committed his life to moving people out of the pews to engage with culture.

Dad always included us kids in his pursuit of seeing lives changed. Frequently on Saturday mornings, he would recruit my younger brother and me to roam the neighborhood in search of Mormons or Jehovah's Witnesses so we could invite them to our house. They would usually come over and have something to eat, spend time with our family, and share spiritual values. Later, when I was a high school student, my dad offered me a group leader role in his ministry, taking students into the inner city to reach out to drug addicts, prostitutes, alcoholics, and the homeless.

Growing up, I had an inherent desire to be a part of something significant—something that would impact lives. Even now, I believe that deep inside each of us is the desire to be a part of something bigger than ourselves. None of us want to spend our days feeling as though our lives have no value, worth, or purpose. But as far as I could see, church was *not* the place to experience something bigger.

As a young adult, I had a few bad church experiences that aligned me with a personal equivalent of the cinematic aphorism "*Hasta la vista*, baby." I wanted nothing to do with organized institutional church or those within it. You know which ones I am talking about—the judgmental, holier-than-thou, self-righteous, don't-take-my-seat (or my front-row parking spot), it's-all-about-me type of churchgoers. I had become a cynic and a doubter of the bride of Christ.

Oddly, though I had become bitter toward insiders, I was neurotic about reaching outsiders—creating an unhealthy dichotomy of expression. I was inviting people into the church while at the same time detesting it. No matter how disappointed and disenchanted I was with Jesus-followers, deep inside I acknowledged that the church was still the collective beacon reflecting Jesus to the world.

I honestly did not possess any resolve to reconcile this dichotomy. Fortunately, for my sake, God began to set in motion a series of contexts that would help sort out this internal tension. One of those contexts would include the academic halls of "Bridal College," or Bible college. Bible college was the last thing on my mind in those days, but because of a knee injury and a lost athletic scholarship, I didn't know what else to do. During my first two years of school I roamed from class to class with no direction or major—unless you count majoring in *Seinfeld* or *The Simpsons*. The nightmare stories of my professors who had once been pastors only solidified my determination never to be a pastor. Of course, my bad attitude toward church didn't stop me from thinking I had all the answers.

Something, though, must have been seeping in during those years. I went from knowing it all to knowing nothing. I began to struggle with big questions. How, I wondered, can I be about God's purpose but not be about his people?

In the opening pages of his book *Soul Cravings*, Erwin McManus writes, "Bitterness is the enemy of love because it makes you unforgiving and unwilling to give love unconditionally. It is the enemy of hope because you keep living in the past and become incapable of seeing a better future."[1]

Bitterness blinded me like being sandblasted in the eyeballs. My bitterness toward the church had kept me from seeing a better future. A future where the very essence of God's people would serve as the catalyst for a movement. I wanted to be a part of this catalyst—something I was discovering to be *community*.

A new paradigm was forming in my head of what church and church ministry could look like. I morphed from a cynic into a dreamer. The cliché that you're either part of the problem or part of the solution challenged me to rethink my faith in conjunction with my real life. For so long I had been sure I didn't want to be a pastor, but I never lost my desire to add value to the world. Once I discovered that being a pastor was the best way for me to make a difference, there was nothing I wanted to be more.

The Plunge into Ministry

In August 1997, my wife, Bernadette, and I were coaching a sports camp in Medford, Oregon. It was a Monday morning when I received the worst possible news. My father had been traveling to speak to a group of Christian leaders when his vehicle was hit head-on by a truck, killing him instantly. The news left me numb and devastated. The shadow of death hovered over the valley in which my safe, comfortable life had existed. Bernadette and I left the camp and headed straight home to Alberta. It took a week before I allowed myself to shed a tear. Attending the memorial was like a surreal combination of high school graduation, family reunion, and church.

A few days later, I was asked to fill in for my dad, taking some of his responsibilities at Prairie Bible College, where he had served as professor of evangelism and apologetics. I could feel my dad's presence as I stood behind his desk. I was honored to step into the role—though doing so was as emotionally painful as it was restorative. Still, I dove into my newfound work. Over the next couple of years, I developed outreach programs and taught classes to college students who were preparing for whatever kingdom endeavor God was calling them to.

I had found a way to talk about the church while avoiding the calling to be in church leadership, but it was only a matter of time before the desire to get my hands dirty kicked in. My pastoral ignorance weighed on me, and I felt God urging me to get involved within ministry leadership.

At first my plan was to take it slowly—part-time and gradually. But God had a different agenda, one that included juggling two new ministry jobs. I was offered a part-time teaching position at Multnomah Bible College in Portland, Oregon; at the same time, I was offered a full-time, one-year associate pastor position at a 125-year-old church in downtown Portland.

Both jobs were challenging in their own way, but it was the church position that posed the most significant challenges. I had great plans to attract people through new programs, a revised vision statement, contemporary worship, relevant sermons, creative bulletins, stylish signs, and gourmet coffee. I was naive and optimistic, and I had a simple strategy—much like a 3:00 a.m. infomercial highlighting a Flowbee, Chia Pet, or Thighmaster. I wanted to make our church the sexiest, most desirable, most enticing thing around. My ideas were on their way to execution—and I had no idea what was in store.

The Plunge into Disillusionment

A short time after my arrival, the church was set to celebrate its 125th anniversary. There was no shortage of memorial plaques, limestone architecture, stained-glass windows, and ornate woodwork to remind you of the church's long history.

The church had a tradition of celebrating its anniversary with the sacred feast known as "the potluck." Each year the members would gather for worship and then proceed downstairs to the fellowship hall for an after-service meal. Immediately I saw an opportunity for our church to engage with the culture around us. I began to set in motion a vision in which the two worlds would collide — with (hopefully) a grand result.

A few days after presenting my idea to the council, the elder who oversaw the missions program contacted me. "If this year's anniversary celebration is going to focus on outsiders," he said, "my wife and I won't be there."

It's so easy to not like Christians.

Maybe it would have been easier to like them if everyone else had been more open to loving their neighbors than this elder was. But they weren't. They made me appreciate the truth of Mark Driscoll's words in *The Radical Reformission*: "As long as Christians fail to repent of self-righteousness, we will continue to speak of evangelism in terms such as *outreach*, which implies that we will not embrace lost people but will keep them at least an arm's length away."[2]

We did have one individual in our church, a Sunday school teacher, who went out of his way to connect with an outsider. This teacher zeroed in on a guest one Sunday morning and said, "If you are going to come in and participate in the service, you need to remove your hat."

We had been working hard to create a culture of acceptance and love for our surrounding community — doing such things as volunteering at the local mission, passing out sandwiches to the hungry, praying with sex addicts, and providing support for drug abusers. After several months of inviting and loving on outsiders, this incident felt like a kick to the groin. For every step forward, it seemed as though we took three steps back.

A few of us didn't give up though. We continued to go out into the community to serve people with various needs. For several weeks I made exciting announcements from the pulpit about the opportunity. The plan was to meet at the church at

7:00 p.m., pray for a few minutes, then go out together. It's one of the most vulnerable and testing places a leader can be. You cast vision, you plan, you commit—and you wait anxiously, hoping people will follow. It is a defining moment for the insecure heart. In my case, the plan didn't work. As 7:30 rolled around, it became obvious that I was being stood up like a bad prom date and that no one would be joining me that evening. My heart sank with shame and disgrace.

My fears had come to pass: I was trying to lead a church toward compassion, and they wouldn't follow. It's the very reason that I never wanted to be a pastor. I was at the end of my rope, and it was time to start making deals with God. (That's usually what we do when we are desperate and out of ideas.) I decided to take a couple of weeks to get away and just pray. I was so hurt and demotivated that I tried desperately to bargain with God. I prayed that some other door would open—that I would find a way out.

By the time I returned from my short season of prayer, it had become clear that I was meant to stay and persevere through whatever God was teaching me. It's not like there was a note from God or a Charlton Heston voice from heaven. It was just a clear, substantial sense of peace. However, staying proved more difficult than I'd imagined. I was facing a battle on two fronts. On the one side, we were attempting to reshape an established church culture; on the other side, I was fighting my own desire to jump ship.

A few months later one of my best friends, Tony, walked into my office and commented on the beams of sunshine that penetrate into my office through the palate of colors in the stain-glassed windows. The sun was particularly vibrant that day. I was glad for the sunshine. I was even gladder that Tony was there. I needed someone to help me process my thoughts, and he was the guy. Tony was someone who believed in me. I knew he would go the distance for me, no matter what I asked.

As we sat there talking—me pouring out my heart, expressing how frustrated I was about the apathy within our church—Tony began to descend into the recesses of my personal "disturbia." I shared how I felt like all I did was put out fires and manage everyone's expectations rather than being released to develop the vision that was in my heart. As the sun set on our conversation, it was undeniable that something needed to change. I have to wonder if that sunset was a divine metaphor for the sun beginning to set on this chapter of my ministry journey.

And then Tony presented a thrilling and disturbing idea. "Have you ever considered planting a new church?" he asked. "Serena [Tony's wife] and I have been thinking about it, and we'd love to have you be the lead pastor."

I wasn't sure how to respond. Would my leaving be considered a failure or opportunity? Was God calling me to something else, or did he want me to stay and persevere?

Bernadette and I struggled with the issue for weeks. I craved the day that I could stop just managing people's expectations and start expressing the portrait of church that was being rendered on my heart, but ultimately I knew I should keep my commitment to the church I was already serving—and I chose to stay. The rest of my tenure there was full of difficulties, and I often wondered if I had made the right choice. But I realize now that my heavenly Father was beaming light on those dark hours of frustration.

And the dream to start a new church had not died.

The Plunge into Dependence on God

The idea of church planting was foggy at first. I wasn't sure I had it in me, but when Tony approached me to discuss the possibility a second time (after my commitment to the other church had ended), I became more and more excited. The thought of starting a church from the ground up was invigorating. It stimulated my entrepreneurial spirit. I wanted to start something new and fresh.

After praying about it, we decided to plant the church in a figurative graveyard. The state of Oregon is considered to be the most unchurched state in the nation. A certain area of Portland is known for churches starting and then dying.

Portland's NW 23rd Avenue, known as "Trendy Third," is a part-upscale, part-bohemian community that could very well be the epicenter of Pacific Northwest style. This urban-forested, pedestrian-friendly district is defined mostly by its shops, restaurants, salons, and cafés, many of which are carved out of elegant old homes. The city's sparkling downtown and artsy Pearl District attract a wide spectrum of people—young and old, rich and poor, pluralistic and highly spiritual. It prides itself on being a culturally enriched area of society.

But even with all that this community had going for it, it was void of a thriving church that fed the hungry souls of spiritual seekers. Perhaps naively, but with a great deal of excitement, we intended to bring to the community the one thing they lacked.

We had a humble beginning, starting with fifteen friends and no money. At the time, my wife and I were living in the suburbs of Portland, fifteen miles from the urban community in which our infant church was located. We were also young novice parents. Our oldest daughter, Mikiah, was three and our son, Jadon, was a newborn. We had bought a fixer-upper just sixteen months earlier, and our weekend-warrior version of a remodel was nearly complete. It was our first home; and in the midst of all the blood, sweat, tears, and elbow grease, it was our little oasis.

One evening, as Bernadette and I were sitting on the living room sofa, she began to let me in on an impression from the Lord that she had been processing. "We can't afford our home so I think we need to sell it and move into the community that we're trying to reach."

"What?" I said, in shock. "This home means so much to you," I added. (Notice how I put the onus back on her.) My immediate response was not in tune with what she was hearing from God. It was a reaction to the beating my tiny little ego was taking. It was hard for me to admit that I was no longer capable of financially providing for my family and our home.

The discussion wasn't over. Tactfully, Bernadette had released only a portion of what she was processing. In complete humility she continued, "I think God wants us to sell our home and all our possessions so that we can invest it into this new church."

I could see the sincerity in what she was suggesting. This moment was a portal into the soul of my wife and her devotion to her Lord and Master. It was awe-inspiring, and I knew that her faith dwarfed mine. I had much to learn from her.

That night we agreed to sell everything that we did not sit on, eat on, or sleep on. It felt hasty and invigorating all at once. Miraculously, our house sold within twenty-four hours. We had enough equity to support us for three months. We had no idea where we were going to live, but we were confident that we were heading in the right direction. Until we could find a place of our own, we stayed with Tony and Serena, who lived in the same neighborhood as our church. We shared meals, partnered in responsibilities, and experienced life together. These were sweet times that would serve as a window into what was to come.

One afternoon, Bernadette and I drove through the community and prayed about a house that we could move into. This particular part of the city was known for its skyrocketing home prices, so buying was not an option. We parked our car alongside the school our church would end up using as a meeting place. As we sat there praying and eating dinner (tightly budgeted peanut butter and jelly sandwiches), one particular home found its way into our entreaties. The house was a pea green, mid-century Tudor converted into a duplex. It was located only a few paces from the school property.

One week later, this very house appeared on the listings as a rental space. Taking this as a direct answer to prayer, we signed the contract and moved in.

We didn't feel we could be a legitimate church until we started offering Sunday morning services, so we rented space in the elementary school across from our home, organized an amazing band, and blanketed the area with marketing. I was convinced if we had an incredible church service, people would flock to us once word started spreading. Looking back, it's easy to see that my expectations were a bit delusional.

Our first Sunday in the school building provided a humbling dose of reality. We were using the school's 1920s-era theatre, which offered a unique atmosphere of urbanity. The entrance to the theatre was flanked by a set of concrete stairs that cascaded into a popular, charming city park. It was a beautiful, sunny day, and our team was anxious. We had everything dialed and were ready to receive our first guests. The service was promoted to start at 10:00 a.m. — not too early and not too late. Perfect. But in that moment I was inundated with feelings that were all too familiar. I stood on those front steps checking my watch every few minutes, vulnerable, again. At 9:50 not a single guest other than our core team of fifteen had walked in. At 9:55 a middle-aged couple entered the building to check us out. At 9:57 a few other people walked in. My anxiety was now magnified by the confirmation that we would start the service with only twenty people.

As I tried to amp myself to speak to this newly launched church, I could barely hold back a sense of rejection that was making me feel devastated. I tried to chalk it up to some opening-day jitters. I didn't want to admit that deep inside I carried a deep wound of rejection that was entangled within my identity and my ministry. If I had been honest, I would have confessed that I blamed the situation on God. What if God were setting me up to fail? What if this were all a part of a heavenly ruse to teach me humility? I walked home that day with my identity, my dreams, and my ideals hanging by a delicate strand of faith.

Weeks passed, and our services remained about as popular as Mr. Furley in his polyester suit at the Regal Beagle. The realization that our little community of faith was not big enough to support our family hit me squarely between the eyes. Of course, this was another blow to my already shrinking ego. I was working long hours, trying everything I could to get this venture off the ground. Still, the church was only able to pay us $500 a month, and that just wasn't going to cut it.

Before long, I ended up in a room full of immigrants and high school dropouts applying for food stamps. Walking through the doors of that government office made me feel like more than just a financial letdown; I was becoming bankrupt in dignity. My self-reliance was stripped away and my motives were exposed. I was angry and thought I was more deserving than anyone else in that room. After all, I had a job (just not a paycheck). I was convinced that everyone else in the room was a deadbeat devoted to abusing the system. In that moment, I was captivated by God's whisper in my heart: "If you are going to pastor this church, then you will have to learn what it means to truly love and not see yourself as better than the ones I am calling you to reach."

I knew what had just taken place. God had smacked me upside the head. I took the whisper of his voice to heart—only to find it was just the beginning of my learning curve. The next lesson for me was the Chihuahua Club.

The Turning Point

Folks in our community had a heightened affection for pets, particularly dogs. It was not uncommon to see a significant number of people out each day with their furry friends. On Sunday mornings, at the exact same time we were having church, a handful of men and women gathered by the school tennis courts with their dogs. After several Sundays, I made an observation about what was happening there: Each of them owned a member of one of the smallest dog breeds in the world, named after a state in Mexico.

I had to know what inspired these folks to get up out of bed early on a Sunday morning to meet. Perhaps they wondered the same thing about us. On my way home from church one day, I approached the chain-link fence that enclosed the tennis courts and addressed a young woman who was throwing a tennis ball to her little friend.

"What's with all the Chihuahuas?" I asked.

"Well, a lot of people around here are nuts about Chihuahuas," she answered.

"You guys come out here every Sunday morning?"

"Yep. We're a little obsessed over them, and we enjoy meeting together. I love this Chihuahua Club."

At first I thought, *To each their own*. But within a few weeks, the club had grown in attendance. They were experiencing more growth than we were.

"My ministry sucks," I told Bernadette. "A little rat dog has more significance in this community than I do."

She laughed and said it wasn't true, but deep inside I think she also knew the bleak reality.

"It doesn't get any lower than this," I'd mutter as I floundered in self-pity. "I rate lower than a dog."

What might have been the perfect recipe for a ministry breakdown actually inspired the revolution of a ministry breakthrough. Reflecting on a missional methodology, I knew there was something to learn from the Chihuahua.

Being hip didn't work.

We had a great Sunday morning service. We put everything we had into it, hiring some of the best musicians in the city for our worship team, offering relevant messages, using creative arts, brewing gourmet coffee, and giving away really cool gifts to our guests (the few that came). Many of my pastor-friends would attend our services because they heard about some of the cool things we were doing. They were surprised we were not busting out of the doors and suggested a supernatural restraint may be standing in the way of our growth. In retrospect I believe that if we had had instant success, exploding from day one, we would never have experienced the real lesson God had for us.

No matter how hip our Sunday service was, it had a serious flaw. It wasn't connecting with the community in which we found ourselves. I came to realize that it wasn't so much the Chihuahuas that motivated people to gather, but the desire to be in community. Their gathering reflected a universal, innate, divinely created *need to belong*. In spite of the rivalry, this group became an inspiration to me — which gave me a more complete picture of what incarnational ministry could look like.

We had made a fatal assumption that what our services offered was just what people in our community were searching for. It wasn't that they weren't interested in spiritual things— quite the opposite, actually. They were hungry for spiritual enlightenment, but they wanted to experience it in the context of relationships, not church services. Once we understood that they were looking for authentic relationships, we understood what we as a church needed to do.

The Ascent

Drastic changes were needed, and I wasn't sure our team would fully support what I had in mind—and I don't think I completely understood what I had in mind. Our new approach would go against everything that seemed conventional in terms of the way in which churches typically start and function. It would also cost us the only financial support we had. With no building, a few dollars, and only a small group of people, my proposed changes would put us out on a limb. They would either define us or destroy us—but we had to take that risk.

"I don't feel like God has called us to plant a church for ourselves," I told my team, "but I think he wants us to start something that will reach this highly unchurched culture. We have to be incarnational."

To do this, we had to change our entire mind-set. I had to move my office to the local coffee shops. We all had to volunteer in the community, pouring all of our resources back into it. More people from our team had to move into the area. We even had to close down our awesome Sunday services and begin meeting in homes.

Things changed for us. Church became a process, not an event. We began meeting people where they were and joining them in their spiritual journey. Our definition of success changed from numbers, buildings, and programs to authenticity, relationship, and life change. We gave up everything with the hopes of gaining anyone. The question was: Did things change for the people we were targeting?

2

process this

Creating a Movement

I saw an interesting T-shirt the other day. It was brown with the silhouette of a white tree. Below the tree were the words "Tree Hugging Dirt Worshipper." The person wearing the shirt may not have been trying to make a statement against God, but it reminded me of how unchurched Oregon was—and of how people long to connect to the spiritual.

People sometimes describe Portland's spiritual darkness as a dismal cloud. I have often wondered if this "cloud" is connected to the Pacific Northwest's pluralistic approach to spiritual discovery. It is a culture where people form their beliefs in much the same way as they place their complicated orders of gourmet coffee. They prefer a personal blending of gray over the black-and-white perception of Christian religiosity.

One afternoon I was walking home from the park near our house when I ran into Katherine, one of the moms from my daughter's school. We made some small talk about moving into the area, then moved on to the fine points of kindergarten society, and finally to the big question: "So, what do you do?"

"I am a pastor," I said with some hesitation, "and we just started a new church in the community."

Katherine's response was instantaneous and direct. "You should know that we don't value churches around here. We value the environment."

I took the bait. "Hmm. I value both. God wants us to value the environment. Actually, he empowered humans to be in charge of the earth and care for it."

Katherine looked surprised, as if discovering for the first time that one of her values actually aligned with something in the Bible. These few words opened the door for Katherine and me to talk about God (whether God was a *she* or *he*, for example) and what our church was hoping to be in the community. It just so happened that our group was organizing a neighborhood cleanup for the next weekend. I encouraged Katherine to join us.

"That sounds great," she said. "I'll even bring some friends." Then she grinned mischievously. "I will help you spread the love, but I won't help you spread the gospel."

Somehow in Katherine's mind there was a sad and heartbreaking disconnect between love and the gospel. Those words of Katherine will be forever etched into my understanding of unchurched culture.

True to her word, Katherine joined us for the neighborhood cleanup. More important, we joined Katherine in her search for God. Over the next several months Katherine and I had significant conversations—in the halls of the school classrooms, at community events, or in the lobby while we waited to pick up our kids at preschool. And Katherine was eager to show up and help with any service project we hosted for the community.

We did not have a growing Sunday morning worship service, and some in our congregation were questioning the relevance of our presence in the community; but we could not deny the value of what was happening in Katherine's life. Even though she was not stepping across the threshold to a Sunday service, Katherine was coming to church. Her life was changing.

Church is not an event; it's a process. We were not leading a church; we were leading a movement.

Forward Motion

Leading a movement is not about how big our buildings are, how large our attendance is, how hip our services are, how many programs we offer, or how sizable our budgets are—although movements may have large followings and plenty of money. Leading a movement is about motion. Movements capture the essence of life change within the context of relationships. A small group of fifteen people, a gathering of two hundred, or a church of ten thousand can all be movements.

Discipleship is a personal journey where each person moves along the spiritual highway at different speeds and from various origin points. Discipleship recognizes that people need access to the highway from wherever they are—but ultimately with the goal that they are intentionally being led to the ultimate destination of knowing Jesus Christ and conforming to his image.

The movement initiated by Jesus prevailed over every organized religious system in existence at the time. While other systems offered people conviction, Jesus offered completeness. Consider the narrative of the woman at the well (John 4). Jesus engaged with someone who was perceived as a societal doormat. Early in their "taboo" conversation, Jesus asked for a drink of water. This would be like you or me plunking down on a street corner and asking a worn-out prostitute for a piece of gum.

Her response: "You are a Jew and I am a Samaritan woman. How can you ask me for a drink?" (John 4:9). (Imagine that prostitute on the street corner saying, "Um, you know I have AIDS, right?")

Jesus didn't blink. "If you knew the gift of God and who it is that asks you for a drink, you would have asked him and he would have given you living water" (verse 10).

Clearly, the woman had no idea she was talking to the very satisfaction of her spiritual longing.

Jesus continued to pierce through the sham of self-deception by offering more purified water. "Everyone who drinks this water will be thirsty again, but those who drink the water I give them will never thirst. Indeed, the water I give him will become in them a spring of water welling up to eternal life" (verses 13 – 14).

They continued talking, and within moments Jesus had exposed her habit of seeking significance in the arms of men.

We human beings are extremely complicated. God often reveals those hidden areas of our lives that we are certain would make him turn away in disgust—and he sees beneath the mess and clutter. He lets us immerse ourselves in the showers of his goodness. Jesus offered the woman at the well—and he offers us—a sweet taste of God's amazing grace. The woman had been searching for significance in six other men, and now Jesus would be the *seventh* man to leave an impression on her—the seventh, of course, representing the biblical idea of completion.

Beneath the surface of this conversation is a powerful example of the forward motion that is waiting to be discovered by each of us. Jesus met the woman where she was geographically, emotionally, and spiritually and led her forward in the process of spiritual development.

The story continues with John's remarkable observation: "Then, leaving her water jar, the woman went back to the town" (verse 28). I love the fact that John included the detail of her leaving the water jar. What an amazing representation of ful-fillment and life change! Immediately after drinking from the fountain of life that Jesus had offered, she returned to her vil-lage to invite others to partake of the same life-giving water. Jesus moved her from social outcast to spiritual includer, mod-eling precisely what the process of forward motion involves.

This kind of personal journey is just what Jesus had in mind when he talked about *making disciples*—a process of movement from unbelief to abundant life. Discipleship begins before con-version and carries through to completion in Jesus Christ. Jesus' approach to making a disciple included a very natural advance-ment: first, the preliminary engagement; second, an invitation to enter into community with that person; and third, a holistic experience of the process of life transfer.

We assume that Jesus walked up to Peter and Andrew, James and John, and they immediately became convinced dis-ciples. We get the impression that they made a decision based on this onetime invitation. Actually, the relationship between Jesus and his disciples involved many decision points along the way. Making disciples was not instantaneous; it was an ongoing process in which Jesus revealed more of his life and the disciples responded to each successive revelation.

Jesus was very strategic when it came to discipleship. He invested in a few people, giving them a savoring taste of who his Father was. His style of ministry was more relational than aca-demic. He pursued common people—even social outcasts—as his closest friends and followers, bringing them into relationship with him and with each other. He led by example and molded his disciples through individual instruction and shared experi-ence. Jesus met these men where they were on their spiritual journey. For three years he transferred his life, his love, and his legacy to them.

The return on Jesus' investment was the life-changing story of ordinary characters into the chronicles of extraordinary cross bearers.

If this kind of discipleship were unleashed in our lives and communities, we might begin to look like the connected network of God's people that Jesus created—a network of people who are finding discipleship and are mobilized for mission, a network of energized people beautifully portraying the life of Christ.

Leading a movement means having a clear process of transformational discipleship. It has to do with integrating this process mind-set into everything our churches are doing, not suggesting it as one of many programs from which people can choose. It means welcoming organic movement, no matter how out of control it may be.

The design of process aligns all resources, ministries, and efforts to work in harmony. The idea is to step back from all the intricacies of church dynamics and see the whole picture. We need to ask these questions:

- Do all our ministry components work in sync to accomplish the same goal?

- Are we hectically managing a complex system of ministries that compete rather than complement?

- Are we intentionally meeting people where they are?

- Do we have an organic process in place to move people toward the life of Christ?

Starting at the End

If I asked you to get in the car and go for a drive with me, you would probably ask, "Where are we going?" I could respond by saying, "We'll be driving five miles west, turn right on Johnson Street, go another three miles until we get to the taco stand, then turn left at the next light." To which you'd most likely respond by staring in disbelief. Why? Because you weren't asking about directions; you were asking about *destination*. The destination determines the direction, not the other way around. In our churches, we can eliminate anything we are doing that does not lead to the destination.

God has established his will for each of us—which is that we would be transformed into the image of his Son, Jesus Christ: "Those God foreknew he also predestined to be conformed to the image of his Son, that he might be the firstborn among many brothers and sisters" (Romans 8:29).

As for our baby church in Portland, we finally caught on to this truth. We quit trying to be the next mammoth supersized church show, and so we were free to embrace our true DNA. At this point, something remarkable began taking place within our group. We realized that God was more interested in who we were than what we were doing. A burden was lifted. We became a thriving church, not because of how many people were gathering, but because of who we were and what we were hoping to become.

A few months into our new experiment, I met Rick and Debbie at one of our community events. They were in their late forties and had reached the life stage of empty nesters. They had been missionaries for years, and they were very familiar with the Bible. They also happened to be going through a tough season of life. Their unmarried daughter had gotten pregnant and decided to move back in with them. Now they were searching for answers to some tormenting questions. Rick was a cool guy, and I really appreciated his transparency so early in our relationship. I invited them to be a part of our faith community, and they were welcomed enthusiastically by the others.

One afternoon, a troubled-looking Rick approached me, wanting to talk. As the two of us rested on the nearest park bench, he began to confess that he had no hope for life or for his future. He wrestled with the classic symptoms of failure, regret, and midlife disappointment. In that moment, the two of us decided to meet on a weekly basis and process this elusive concept of hope. Sometimes we met over lunch, other times over a game of tennis. (Rick was good. It was like Forest Gump versus Steve Urkel. I was Urkel. But at least I was taking my turf back from the Chihuahuas.) Sometimes I would share passages of Scripture, but it wasn't like I was saying anything that Rick had not heard already. He would agree with everything I was saying, but the look in his face revealed a hopelessly wounded heart.

Over time, Rick and Debbie became part of our community and found their sense of belonging in a group of friends who loved them and wanted to be a part of something divinely unique with them.

At this point in our church's life, we were meeting in our home. We were eating meals together, spontaneously praying together, serving together, laughing and celebrating together. We were opening Scripture with each other. We were hurting together and striving to meet each other's needs. We were welcoming others to join us. We were even building an orphanage in Rwanda together. We had become a village of people, and it was beautiful and energizing, without any pretense or sensationalism. It was perfectly natural. The chemistry and the bonds that were formed united us in a spectacular cohesion of common purpose. We had a commitment to an expression of authentic love. We had become a family, and yet we were part of something bigger than ourselves.

The DNA of this community had touched each of us, especially Rick and Debbie. Rick found a renewed sense of passion for life and his family. After dinner one summer evening, I heard a gentle knock at the front door. Rick had come over to share something from his heart. It was a tranquil evening, and the two of us sat outside on the front steps as Rick revealed what was stirring within.

"Before I came here, I felt like a man on an island surrounded by failure and regret—with no sense of hope or drive," he said. "I had let down my family and God. But being a part of this community has given me a group of friends who pick me up and carry me. It has showed me what a church should look like."

Rick's story isn't that unusual or spectacular, but it sums up what we all felt. Each of us had our own issues of regret, failure, and shame. But being part of something so significant drew us to something above and beyond those things that weighed us down. We could see the destination.

It felt so reminiscent of how Jesus did ministry. Out of a small group of followers Jesus created an amazing community of soul-journers who came together to be part of something bigger than themselves—something that was impacting their culture and astonishing the spiritual realm. They knew where they were going. They could see the destination.

Moving Together

Forward motion toward the designated destination happens best in an environment where people are connected, at those times when it is clear that people are more important than programs.

Yet much of our focus today can be program driven. And no wonder. Program-driven ministries are the perfect product for a consumer culture. People today choose their churches based on which programs are offered. It seems natural to try meeting individuals' felt needs through well-crafted programs—much like a fast-food drive-through.

This was once my ministry MO. I would start by identifying the felt needs and wants of a target audience. Then I would access the church's resources and develop a marketing strategy to recruit volunteers and promote the appropriate opportunity to the target group. I tried to address as many felt needs as possible—which led to overwhelming expectations to provide staff and resources for these programs.

Sometimes programs were put on life support, and people became overwhelmed trying to keep them running. People started feeling pressured to get involved and carry so many responsibilities that they had no time to develop meaningful relationships. Programs became valued more than people. More often than not I felt as though I needed to keep up with the popular programs other churches were offering. But being about people requires that we be OK with not offering every program under the sun. Being about people isn't about doing more, but doing less. Now we try to remove the expectation of having a full ministry calendar so we can experience instead a full release of time to invest in each other.

In a program-driven ministry we find expectations created and communicated to those both inside and outside the church. The message is loud and clear: "Church is all about what you can get out of it." This is dangerous and risky. Often we end up playing a game of bait and switch. In an effort to be attractive and relevant, we portray Jesus as something from an episode of *I Dream of Jeannie.* We skew people's picture of Jesus, leaving them to conclude that God is all about them and therefore church should be all about them too. Then we labor tirelessly, trying to transform them into selfless martyrs for the cross.

Jesus never used gimmicks to draw people into his community. He explained clearly that the pathway to spiritual growth and completeness comes as a result of surrender, not self-seeking ambitions. Jesus disclosed the mystery to this paradoxical certainty to his disciples one afternoon. I imagine Jesus in a scene from the movie *Gladiator.* The character Maximus speaks to his men prior to the battle with the barbarians: "Brothers, what we do in life echoes in eternity." Here Jesus assembles his cherished brothers to hear the maxim of eternity: "Whoever finds their life will lose it, and whoever loses their life for my sake will find it" (Matthew 10:39). I can hear the ricochet of murmurings over this profound statement.

If we are to intersect our faith with real life, we have to stop looking at people as products. People do not fit into nicely organized boxes, but they do fit into organic relationships.

Always Moving

LifeWay Community Church was far from changing the world, but movement was happening and lives were being transformed, including my own. I began to understand that time invested in people resulted in people investing in the kingdom. Yet this raised a new issue. It had taken all I had to invest in a couple dozen individuals. How was I going to do that with the entire church, now that it was growing? I started to rethink everything I did and how I could create an infrastructure of influence with relationship at the core. I didn't want something programmatic; I wanted something personal, yet strategic and intentional as well.

On the brink of taking the next step in our ministry evolution, I came face-to-face with a reality that would alter the course of our lives. One evening, as Bernadette and I were sitting in the living room, she shared an internal struggle she had been battling. She invited me in to the source of her despair, speaking with tears in her eyes: "I can't do it. I need a break from it all."

All the years of pouring out and sacrificing had finally caught up to her. Bernadette felt shame just bringing it up, as if somehow she was sabotaging what God was doing. Actually, she was just being honest with herself and with me. At first I wanted to deny her feelings and try convincing her that it was just a season that would pass. My ambition can sometimes be to my detriment. Sometimes I forge ahead without glancing back to see how others are doing. In reality, I did not want to stop because I was worried that people would see it as *my* failure. At that moment, I think I would have used Jedi mind tricks to change her mind if I could. But eventually (longer than it should have taken), I realized that I was standing at a crossroads: Either I could keep us on the same path and force my wife to experience burnout, or I could slow down and start moving in a different direction.

Right at that time, my pastor-friend James Allison invited me to have lunch with him. We'd had a few conversations over the years, so I thought we were just meeting to catch up. James, however, proposed the idea that I join him on staff at his church, Grace Chapel in Wilsonville, a suburb of Portland. I was surprised by his request, and quite honestly, I wasn't interested in moving back to the suburbs.

A few weeks passed, and I put his proposition on the back burner—until he called again to talk some more. In this second conversation, our hearts blended together as we dreamed of what a church could look like. If only I had known then the friend and brother I would discover in James! He is the strongest and most encouraging pastor I have met. "Take the vision of what you are doing and implement it here," he said to me. It was one of the most empowering and affirming things I've ever been told.

Making the transition from one church to the other proved amazing, and yet we all grieved as we said good-bye to LifeWay Community Church. Some joined other churches and some followed us to our new church. There was so much that we had learned in our church-planting journey, and now we were excited to use all we discovered to make a difference in our new church home. I think I may have been most eager to implement the concept of seeing church as a process that moves people "from community to community"—from the culture in which we live to authentic, missional small groups.

Today, everything we do is about moving people from community to community. The process recycles itself in a circular motion as people engage with the outside community and walk with them relationally through the whole process. As they do, they begin to experience momentum, as well as a sense that they are now part of a movement, not just a church.

Throughout those difficult yet inspiring years at our former church plant, we realized that people are at different stages of their spiritual journeys. We discovered that most people find themselves within various connecting points of community. Some connect around shared needs, some around shared experiences, and others around shared questions.

Familiar Places

Focusing on people rather than programs may seem like a no-brainer, but it requires intentionality. Church leaders must provide natural entry points for relational communication. At Grace Chapel, we accomplished this by identifying three environments in which relationships can take place: the park, the

coffee shop, and the living room. These three environments provide the organic framework for moving people from community
to community—whether it's in a trendy urban neighborhood or
a friendly suburban community. The church encourages community by tapping into these three irresistible environments.

We aren't the first church to talk about creating environments. My friend Bill Willits at North Point Community Church
has significantly influenced my view of relational environments.
While our modern culture helped me focus on these three environments (we seem to find coffee shops on every corner), what
really inspired me was a friendship with a guy named Don.

Don is an eccentric middle-aged man who reminds me of
Jack Nicholson in *As Good as It Gets*. I first met Don in the
park as he was walking his canine companion. I don't know why
I felt the impulse to strike up a conversation, but I did. Maybe
it was because I noticed that his dog looked remarkably similar
to the dog named Lobo I had in my childhood. (Now that I
think about it, more than one of my ministry ideas originated
from people with dogs. Maybe I should have been a vet.) After
talking about the coincidental similarities between our four-
legged friends, Don asked about my vocation. Downplaying the
fact that I was pastor, I returned the question. Don had been
a successful real estate broker for most of his life and was now
experiencing a time of transition.

It was a random conversation until Don began to share some
personal dilemmas he was facing. As our conversation shifted to
a personal and spiritual direction, it became obvious that Don
was searching for God and asking some sincere questions. After a
couple of hours had quickly passed, I made an offer to Don: "If you
ever want to grab some coffee and continue our discussion, just let
me know." Handing him my business card (thank you, Kinkos!),
we said our farewells and went off in different directions.

Later that week, I received a call from Don. He'd decided to take me up on my offer. Within a couple of days, we were continuing our dialogue as we indulged in a couple of tall mochas. Over time, what started as a random meeting turned into stimulating, routine encounters. In an environment where people ordered tall, hot drinks we had our own tall order to meet. Don and I were confronting the inner demons that tormented his heart. Several months passed, and Don started coming to church. (The first time he came, he brought his dog. I didn't have the heart to tell him that he couldn't bring him in. A couple of times during the service his dog crawled under the seats and "flirted" with other people's legs. Really distracting!)

I wanted to go beyond our usual meetings at our favorite neighborhood coffee shop, and so Bernadette and I invited Don to come over for dinner. There is something more personal about inviting someone into your home for a meal. It speaks of relational connectedness and transparency. Sitting in our living room after dinner, I realized how far we had come since the day we sat on that bench in the park.

Over time, three relational environments—the park, the coffee shop, and the living room—gave Don and me the opportunity to connect and journey together in a spiritual pursuit. What's more, the experience forged an image in my mind of how a relational process can be depicted. What if the church modeled its ministry after this image? What if we created these three relational environments, allowing people to connect with those in our community and walking with them through a similar process?

It wasn't just about getting Don to attend church; it was about seeing our relationship grow and our lives change with each step of the journey. At Grace Chapel, we use the metaphors of the park, coffee shop, and living room to explain the environments we have created to engage with people in our community and walk with them through the relational and spiritual process of following Christ. Our vision is about more than just providing a place for people to connect; it's about providing a place for people to experience *completion in Christ*. It makes our church more than just a Sunday morning event as we seek to engage the culture and journey together beyond Sundays.

The Park

One of the most natural environments where community takes place is the park. When you think of a park, you can imagine people gathering around barbecue grills, throwing Frisbees, and enjoying activities together. The park environment at Grace Chapel is where people usually experience our community for the first time—and where we connect with those in our community for the first time—whether it's through a service project, a neighborhood event, or a weekend service.

The Coffee Shop

It seems that when you want to spend time getting to know someone in a comfortable environment, you end up in a local coffee shop. Between sips you begin to connect with people and form friendships. At Grace Chapel, our coffee shop environment— smaller and more interactive than the park—creates opportunities for friendships to be forged. These spaces may take the form of retreats, social events, or even global missions trips.

The Living Room

Imagine spending quality time over the course of several visits to the coffee shop. Before you know it, you're inviting your new friends to come over to your house. When they arrive, generally you invite them into the living room first. Have you ever thought about the extraordinary occurrences that can take place when you do ordinary activities? For instance, has it crossed your mind that the simple act of taking out your garbage holds the possibility of opening the door to something life-changing? In our neighborhood, garbage pickup was on Tuesday mornings. I know this because I proudly carry the mantle of "Rubbish Annihilator." I see taking out the garbage as a true husband's job. It's a fact of life, and I don't fight it.

One particularly warm Monday evening, I was fulfilling my husbandly role of vanquishing the dark villain of spoil. (If it helps, imagine me wearing one of those awesome lucha libre wrestling masks). As I boldly tossed the refuse to the curb, my fellow grime fighter, Chris (better known as our neighbor), approached me. Standing there in triumph, we began to chatter about the toils of the day. Only a few seconds slipped by before Chris admitted that he had lost his job a few days earlier. I've seen that look before—the look of a man losing his dignity and now feeling nothing but fear and despondence. That night, Bernadette and I decided to invite Chris to move in with us until he found a job. Chris slept on the couch, ate meals with us, hung his clothes in the closet, and set up his computer on the dining room table. I'll never forget the late nights when Chris and I would talk about God, life, and wine. (Chris had been a wine distributor.) Chris would also come to church with us on the weekend. One month later, he found a job in another state and moved away.

I always wondered what impact we had on Chris—that is, until I received a letter a few months later. Chris acknowledged that he had seen a side of God that he had never experienced before. He mentioned our honest, open conversations about spiritual questions. To him, our living room had become a sacred space into which God could enter and change lives.

At Grace Chapel, we believe that life happens in the living room. Within the living room environment, we have home groups (which we call Life Groups). Ultimately, we want everyone to have the experience of being in a Life Group. This is where lasting friendships are made. It's a safe place to open your heart, share your life, and ask tough questions. It's about commitment, strength, and love. In a self-centered society like ours, the home can be more than just a place of solitude; it can become a place of solace for souls. Getting there is the journey I'll describe in the following chapters. But before we go forward, let me say one more thing. There is a risk to faith in real life, and you need to ask yourself an important question: What is God asking you to do with it? I hope our journey will help you fill in the blanks.

3

mad dogs and gladiators

Aligning Goals

In those naive early years of ministry, I experienced one of the most common expressions of church. The setting was a small church entrenched in its traditional ethos. The lead pastor and I had been working hard to help this long-established church become more effective at reaching its broad, eclectic, progressive community.

Initially we were embraced as leaders who were making positive changes and adding a fresh touch to what everyone agreed was a stale environment. We were seeing numerical growth—not to mention the amazing spiritual growth experienced by those who traded in their legalistic religiosity for a newfound, grace-centered spirituality.

But with each change we made came the growing belief that we were tampering with the sacred and consecrated relics from a time past. As outsiders began filling the pews and threatening the status quo, the changes were increasingly challenged with opposition, criticism, and resentment from insiders. Board meetings, congregational meetings, and volunteer meetings were infamous for fist-slamming, voice-raising, and insult-hurling character assassinations. Just imagine the

Jerry Springer circus minus the transsexuals and paternity tests.

And then it happened. A group of individuals compelled to guard their church heritage formed their own leadership team. Their prime objective was to reestablish the church as they knew it. I met with them — hoping to curtail their determined focus. I will never forget the lonely feeling of sitting in that musty room. I sat gazing across the large formal oak table as six intimidating individuals stared back at me with hollow, disappointed eyes. (I felt like Marty in *Back to the Future Part III* when he was facing Buford "Mad Dog" Tannen in a dual at high noon. I swear I could hear the whistling main theme of *The Good, the Bad and the Ugly* lingering in the background.) With no agreement or acquiescence in sight, these church members simply slid their chairs back and walked out of the meeting. Within a short while, the church became a fractured, wounded victim of disunity.

When the church cannot get on the same page, sideways energy is exerted — which is always costly and detrimental to movement and to the cause of Christ. It becomes like rust, corroding the church and causing it to grind to a halt.

I am reminded of the comments of Paul as he aspired to get members of the Corinthian church on the same page with one another: "I appeal to you, brothers and sisters, in the name of our Lord Jesus Christ, that all of you agree with one another in what you say and that there may be no divisions among you, but that you be perfectly united in mind and thought" (1 Corinthians 1:10).

The fundamental question all leaders ask is, How do we get the people to move in the direction that we desire? It starts with alignment.

Alignment with Calling

When I was involved in church planting, my friend and mentor Randy would tell me that God begins a church by planting one in the heart of a pastor. Church planting is the messy, usually muddled process of transferring what's on the heart into reality.

Often, leading a church gets reduced to the day-to-day obligations of ministry responsibilities and going through the motions. If we aren't careful, routine responsibilities can overshadow and eclipse the unique calling and vision that God wants to grow from what he has planted in our hearts.

The first few paragraphs of Nehemiah reveal the calling God planted in his heart:

> The words of Nehemiah son of Hakaliah:
>
> In the month of Kislev in the twentieth year, while I was in the citadel of Susa, Hanani, one of my brothers, came from Judah with some other men, and I questioned them about the Jewish remnant that had survived the exile, and also about Jerusalem.
>
> They said to me, "Those who survived the exile and are back in the province are in great trouble and disgrace. The wall of Jerusalem is broken down, and its gates have been burned with fire."
>
> When I heard these things, I sat down and wept. For some days I mourned and fasted and prayed before the God of heaven.
>
> NEHEMIAH 1:1–4

Nehemiah's vision was birthed as a result of aligning his heart with God. This is a powerful and vulnerable insight into the character of Nehemiah. You can imagine the agony and anguish of his heart coming into alignment—formed in the midst of his humility, confession, weeping, prayer, and brokenness.

Leading a movement is about aligning our time, our values, our resources, and our strategies with God's divine plan for our lives and our churches.

Most leaders would love to do that. In fact, they probably wish their congregations would release them to align these elements. However, far too often they get preoccupied with sideways energy, prohibiting them from focusing their efforts where they are really being led. Aligning a church around the vision God has given inevitably leads to conflicts, battles, and risk taking. The key is to fight the right battles—to know which risks to take, and at all times to align with what God is birthing in our hearts. Unfortunately, all too often I've found myself battling and risking for things I don't care about or am not confident that God wanted me to invest in.

Leading a movement involves adjusting objects in relation to each other, with the goal of helping them work harmoniously for a greater good. It sounds easy, but it's not. The process of adjusting and readjusting people's opinions, experiences, and expectations into the overall vision causes doubt and continual second-guessing. Yet our confidence is anchored in the assurance of God's calling. Being firmly rooted in a God-originated vision is essential. It gives us the fortitude to boldly say, "This is what God called us to be"—and then lovingly, patiently, even courageously, calling others to follow.

A few weeks ago, I was talking with the pastor of a large church in our area. Having made ourselves comfortable in his office, we began sharing the dreams God had put on our hearts. Within minutes, I became fascinated by the similarities of our strategies, thoughts, and perspectives on ministry. It was surreal to hear the words come out of his mouth as though they were being picked out of my own mind. But for him, this exciting vision represented a drastic change of course for his church. I had to ask, "How did you get your church aligned around this new direction?"

By the look in his eyes, I could tell that the answer was going to be very complex. Indulging my inquiry, he dove in. "I started by sharing with the elders that God had put something on my heart and that I needed to be obedient to it." The elders meeting was a defining moment. The pastor told them that if they did not believe this new direction was best for the church, then he would seek to replace himself with a pastor who was a better fit for them. His love for this church and close relationships allowed him to be honest without coming across as though a gun was being held to their heads. Casting vision with the invitation for others to join isn't about coercion; it's about honesty and obedience. I am convinced that without the understanding and devoted relationship he shared with these men over the years, he would not have had the freedom to lay his cards on the table.

The deep conviction that God was stirring inside him led him to be honest with himself and his elders. Remarkably, they responded with affirmation and promised to support him as the church worked toward the necessary transition and alignment.

"That was what gave me the confidence to move forward and bring the rest of the church into alignment," he said. I could only imagine the daunting task of turning such a large ship. I pressed for more.

"I stood before the congregation," he said, "and as boldly as I could, I shared my heart for our church's new direction."

The majority of people supported the new direction, but many also left.

The next step was even more radical. The pastor asked everyone on staff to resign and then reapply for what position they thought would best fit them in this new direction.

I could hardly believe it.

"We had too many people sitting in the wrong seats on the bus, and we needed to get our staff into alignment with the new direction," he said. In the end, they lost only two staff members in the transition and had a much stronger, more deeply invested team.

Alignment has to start at the top. It's astonishing to think about the process this pastor led his church through. He took some bold steps with himself, his elders, his congregation, and his staff. And it all began with his own soul-searching to discover what God was calling him to, and then obediently laboring to help others embrace that same vision.

Momentum happens when a leader moves with spiritual integrity and urgency in response to the call that God has given. When we have an unmistakable impression of God's calling, combined with submission to God's Spirit and connected to a clear vision, movement begins to accelerate. Leading a movement happens best when we realize we are ultimately leading a community with a cause or mission—when we understand that what God has birthed in our hearts is meant to be shared and embraced by the rest of the community. We have to understand the sacrifice of what it will cost us (and others) as we move forward.

Aligning people with the vision that God has planted in our hearts requires us to stop functioning like CEOs and take on the role of servants. Movements are not led by people who depend on the sacrifices of others. People do not want to follow a delegator; they want to follow a demonstrator. Delegation has its place, but leading a movement is, first and foremost, about running the race and calling others to run alongside us. Being in front is not just about forward thinking; it's about forward living.

This type of leadership is illustrated in my all-time favorite movie, *Gladiator*. General Maximus Decimus Meridius rises through the ranks of the gladiatorial arena, accompanied by a following of loyal comrades. His ability to move others is captured in his heroic proclamation as the rusted gates of the citadel unbolt: "You can help me. Whatever comes out of these gates, we've got a better chance of survival if we work together. Do you understand? If we stay together, we survive." The picture of alignment is clear as they form a military phalanx moving in perfect formation and emerge victorious.

Leading a movement will not happen if people do not move together in common cause with the leader as their exemplar.

Alignment with Purpose

What is the purpose of the church? Some say it's evangelism; some say glorifying God, feeding on the Word, enjoying God together, making disciples, being a house of prayer; some say creating Christian community, and so on. So what is it? The answer is both complicated and simple.

The complicated answer is that it's all of the above and more. The simple answer can be given in just one word: *respond*.

The purpose of the church is to respond to God's revelation. It's that simple. Respond to the cross, respond to God's word, respond to his Spirit, and respond to the life of his Son. When the church responds to God's revelation, we inevitably live out our divine purpose.

Even Jesus stated that his mission was a response to his relationship with the Father. The evening before his execution, he said, "Father, if you are willing, take this cup from me; yet not my will, but yours be done" (Luke 22:42). Before Jesus did any ministry, he aligned himself with the Father and the Holy

Spirit. No greater fuel will ignite a movement of God's people than the internal blaze of God's revelation through the power of his word and his Spirit.

The difference between leading a church and leading a movement is that with the former, you're aspiring to help people align their hearts in response to God's revelation.

But there's also a difference between the *mission* of the church and its *purpose*. The mission of the church is the action, whereas the purpose is the reason for the action. But we have to be careful. In our modernistic efforts to explain and define the purpose of the church, we may inadvertently reduce it to a handful of systems. Many churches today are experiencing the curse of modernism's obsession with formulas and methodology. It has become possible to respond to systematic itemizations such as prayer meetings, Bible studies, worship gatherings, and mission trips without actually responding to God. A church may appear to be living out the purpose of the church, but their motives can be contrived and artificial.

Now, I know from experience the danger in this way of thinking about motives. It can lead people to constantly question motives, trying to decipher if our expressions of faith are sincere or just symptomatic of going through the motions. It's not that we want people debilitated by frequent second-guessing about whether they are responding to God or to the words of someone who told them what's expected of a Christian.

I love how Paul came to his conclusion on motives when writing to the Philippians:

> It is true that some preach Christ out of envy and rivalry, but others out of goodwill. The latter do so out of love, knowing that I am put here for the defense of the gospel. The former preach Christ out of selfish ambition, not

sincerely, supposing that they can stir up trouble for me while I am in chains. But what does it matter? The important thing is that in every way, whether from false motives or true, Christ is preached. And because of this I rejoice.

PHILIPPIANS 1:15–18

Paul doesn't seem to mind what the motives are, as long as the message of Christ is being communicated. Neither do I. I am simply cautioning against encouraging people to respond to a program rather than to a Person in our attempts to align others around the purpose of the church. In all of our efforts to be "purpose driven," we must be careful not to lead others simply to go through the motions without really engaging in a love affair with God. Jesus illuminated this same caution as he warns the church in Ephesus that they "have forsaken the love [they] had at first" and that they should "do the things [they] did at first" (Revelation 2:4, 5).

Alignment with Mission

Have you ever had one of those painfully humbling moments of enlightenment? That split-second realization that who you are is not as noble as you think you are? It seems I have these moments more often than I'd like. One Saturday early in my ministry years, Bernadette and I were enjoying a stroll through the mall. After window-shopping at the Gap and testing the leather massage chairs at Sharper Image, we found ourselves dining on the delicacies at the food court. Indulging on the cornucopia of fried cuisine and Orange Julius, we ignored the commotion of the nearby shoppers. Beneath the backdrop of neon lights and multiple food vendors, a middle-aged woman dressed in a cobalt uniform approached a garbage can only a few feet from our table. Barely noticing her presence, I whispered in a conceited breath, "I am so glad I'm not that woman." Honestly, something arrogant and sinister came from deep within.

That split second I had made an atrocious inference. How shallow of me to presume her identity and worth were based on her employment! For someone trained in the art of preaching the cross, I had failed miserably at recognizing the value that the cross awarded to this individual. Instantly I felt that all of my so-called faith was a sham. Humbled by this realization, I began to pray that God would align my heart with his and that I would begin to see people the way he sees them.

What does this story have to do with the mission of the church? Everything! It's impossible to be on track with God's mission when we omit his perspective on people. Much has already been written on mission alignment between postmodernism and the emerging church. I have had my share of microbrewed, pub-stimulated emerging church conversations about the new ways of being the church or "church next." My thoughts are not intended to be a textbook on either of these themes but more of a personal journey in response to them. If I've learned anything from emerging leaders, it's that we must be willing to lose all forms in order to embrace a faith that will thrive in real life.

What the church needs today is not a new fad or trendy makeover. Rearranging the furniture, adding candles, or wearing untucked metro shirts (I have a proud collection of metro shirts that suit my style—no pirate shirts with ruffles, though!) will not change our perspective of how we see people. It's certainly not the solution to reaching a post-Christian, postmodern, post-postmodern, or post-whatever culture. What the church needs to do is experience a paradigm shift that recaptures the vintage missiology on which it was founded. A sister church in our city, Imago Dei Community, led by my friend Rick McKinley, traces their mission alignment back to an evening of confession. This act of repentance stemmed from not having an authentic love for the broken people in the city.

Most churches today must reestablish their mission. This will not happen by simply rearranging the furniture and coming up with a new marketing campaign. In the words of missional leadership specialist Reggie McNeal, "The North American church is suffering from severe mission amnesia. It has forgotten why it exists."[3] Reestablishing mission can happen only when those in the church as individuals align their lives around the exact mission of Jesus Christ, when they adopt an "it's not about me" attitude and embrace the "missio Dei"—exemplified in these words of Jesus: "Peace be with you! As the Father has sent me, I am sending you" (John 20:21).

The sending of God (or mission of God) is birthed out of God's very nature. God by his character is a sending (or missional) God. He is the author and initiator of his desire to redeem humanity back into a *shalom* (undivided peace-filled) relationship with himself. He planned the incarnation of his Son for this purpose, and today he sends the church into the world, equipped with the gospel for the same result. This undertaking is a movement of God where the church is valued as a chosen vessel used for the effecting of God's purpose. To be mission focused is to participate in the movement of God. This is God's redemptive story, with the cross as the centerpiece. Our aspiration as the church is to align ourselves within God's redemptive story. Finding ourselves in this divine narrative is the core expression of what it means to be a missional church.

A church that does missions and a missional church are radically different entities. This difference establishes the foundation and determines the strategy and vision for a church. Being a missional church is not about having a missions program; it's about making the ministry of reconciliation (see 2 Corinthians 5:18) central to all of its ministries.

At the core of being missional is Jesus' Great Commission to "go and make disciples" (Matthew 28:19). And the best way to summarize the dynamic of making disciples is with the word *process*. Again, there is a misalignment in the church when we separate "reaching out" and "raising up." You can often sense the tension that's created when people restrict their focus to one option or the other. The mandate to make disciples was intended to be a collective effort between reaching out and raising up. They work in tandem, bringing to completion Jesus' vision for the spiritual formation of individuals. Missional alignment happens as each ministry department organizes itself around the principle of process, including the fluid motion between reaching out and raising up.

The very essence and identity of the missional church are modeled after the incarnational example of Jesus. Just as the fullness of God became flesh and integrated within humanity's earthly context, so the missional church must integrate itself within a cultural context for the sake of the world. The church, then, is made up of God's sent people—which means that wherever God's people exist, there is the church in its sent form. Alignment happens as the church rediscovers and engages with what it means to be God's sent people. They explore and learn what it looks like to be sent as Jesus was sent.

The college I attended was known for its missions focus and its legacy of sending students around the globe. During one commissioning service in the auditorium, a well-known missionary addressed us. His message was stirring and inspiring, but his conclusion troubled me. After an inspiring message about "going into the world," he invited students to respond by standing up if they intended to take the gospel to some other part of the world. He said, "Stand up if you feel the call to go to Africa." Then he continued, "Those of you who feel the call to go to China, stand up." Continents and countries were rattled off, as students stood proudly to symbolize their response to God's calling. The auditorium was filled with hundreds of students standing as one. I waited eagerly for North America's turn, anticipating my opportunity to declare my desire to be a missionary in our homeland. Every continent was mentioned—except North America. I sat there feeling ashamed that I was not participating in overseas missionary activity. I am sure his omission wasn't intended to overlook North America but deep down, I was a little angry that he had neglected to mention one of the most challenging cross-cultural areas of the globe.

Somehow we think that getting on a plane to host a children's camp in Africa is doing missions, while hosting a Sunday morning children's program at home is just "doing church." It is a mistake to lose sight of the fact that the church—wherever it may be—is God's missional vehicle for redeeming the world. Intersecting our faith with real life is about recapturing the church's missional identity.

Sometimes I hear that a church designates 10 percent of its budget for "missions," as if it prides itself on being aligned with God's true heartbeat. This type of thinking can be confusing to the overall ministry of the church. Ironically, it places this specific church further out of alignment with God's understanding of missiology and ecclesiology. Think about it. We don't set aside 10 percent for children's ministry or youth ministry, yet those involved in those areas are actually doing missions work. The missions budget of a church should be defined as the general budget of the church. Some may consider it a matter of semantics, but categorizing a budget line item as "missions" only adds to the confusion.

Alignment happens as the church abandons its role as a self-help institution and embraces its identity as a missionary movement. At the very core of the ancient church was the nucleus of a missional movement. This shift requires a new methodology that is bold, creative, and innovative. These shifts imply the recalibration of ancient values.

Alignment with Culture

Missionaries understand the importance of aligning their strategy with their cultural environment. They understand that they must have an accurate insight into the surrounding culture before they create, develop, and execute a strategy within that context.

Likewise, if a church is to align itself with its missional heritage, it must ask itself this question: What is the ministry shape that God is calling us to in this particular cultural context? This is a significant question, because the missional church has to be relevant within its cultural context in order to play its part in God's redemptive story.

Alignment with culture is a fluid and adaptable process. As culture changes, our methodology must shift with it. This cultural alignment causes many churches to appear so radical and unconventional that they bear no resemblance to church as we know it. Aligning with culture, of course, can be tricky. The goal is to incarnate ourselves within culture without being seduced by it — to be in the world, but not of it (see John 17:14 – 18).

Many churches are intimidated by the drastic implications of aligning with culture. They refuse to make the changes and shifts necessary to keep up with their cultural milieu. But change is inevitable. If a church refuses to align itself with the surrounding culture, it becomes irrelevant.

Change and alignment are synonymous. Alignment suggests a continual process of change—that is, frequently assessing one's heart, perspective, methodology, and strategy. The antithesis to change is maintenance—or worse, atrophy. Many churches today are stuck in the mire of maintenance, hindering them from cultivating momentum.

Even though we all know that God does not change in his character, we can still argue for a theology of change. Consider the change from the old covenant to the new covenant, old wine/old wineskins to new wine/new wineskins, or the old self and old creation to the new self and new creation. The Bible provides a practical theology of change—one that can be seen, for example, in the book of Isaiah, who quotes the Lord: "See, I am doing a new thing! Now it springs up; do you not perceive it?" (43:19).

The church is indigenous to its cultural background. As the postmodern storm blows westward, it turns over the pages of modernity and its influence on the church. A new cultural chapter is being written, and the missional church has the honor of emerging as the next dramatic chapter inked in the pages of church history. This shift in the wind will bring about a monumental reforming of church as we know it.

In their book *The Shaping of Things to Come*, Michael Frost and Alan Hirsch describe this "epoch-shifting period":

> There is every indication that this cultural shift will be even more profound and radical than was the shift precipitated by the Renaissance, which took place within the auspices of Christendom. What is happening now is entirely outside of any discernable Christian influence. We propose that what

will emerge from the chaos of the current social-historical shift to the postmodern is likely to be a second reformation as the church rediscovers itself as an apostolic movement. In fact, we suggest that if the church in the West does not embrace such a radical recalibration, it will find itself increasingly imperiled.[4]

To be honest, at first I felt threatened by this new wave of cultural change. Everything inside of me wanted to stay put and ride out the storm. However, I have discovered many beautiful aspects to this prevailing squall. No longer do I stand on the bow of my ship, cursing the perfect storm; instead I respect its fury. When observed from a dry viewpoint, the fury seems far removed. However, by taking the risk of becoming engulfed, we gain the opportunity to align our missional strategy in order to harness the rage. We merge our faith with real life.

Quite honestly, my paralyzing fear was driven by the need for control and self-preservation. I had worked hard to create a place where everyone had to come to God on my terms. I had drawn the lines, and I wanted everyone else to color inside them. When they did, it affirmed my ego; when they didn't, it threatened to undermine my theology and ultimately my identity. When I first started teaching at Multnomah Bible College, I was assigned to teach a class called Anthropology, Christology, and Soteriology—or ACS for short. Over time, the students and I developed a great rapport. I was flattered by the post-lecture feedback they would share as we exited the classroom.

One of my favorite students was a guy named Ryan. He didn't grow up in the church. In fact, he'd led a rather intense street life. The intimidating tattoo on Ryan's head, just beneath his buzz cut, attested to his tough upbringing. Talking with Ryan was always enjoyable because he would acknowledge everything

I had just covered. Before long, Ryan and many other students like him wound up sitting in our living room for a weekly small group. We sang songs, hung out, and talked about God. It was easy. When you're preaching to the choir, the chances of being threatened are minimal. It just feels so comfortable.

On the opposite end of the spectrum, a few years later I found myself engaging with students at Portland State University, just a block away from our downtown church. Students here did not take a liking to Christianity, and they certainly did not approach spirituality from my perspective. Their approach to God included experimenting with all sorts of spiritual venues. Their advance to spiritual enlightenment just wasn't as linear as mine. Our conversations felt more like abstract compositions. They were neither affirming nor comfortable. Every theological viewpoint I outlined was challenged. Deep down, I was a little afraid they would ask a question or say something that would shatter my carefully constructed, neatly organized theology. They wanted to color outside the lines. Organizing a quaint Bible study and singing worship songs weren't going to work with this crowd. It demanded something other than my self-affirming codependency. I had to get over my fear of discomfort and allow them the space they needed to pursue God from a subjective viewpoint.

When our five-year-old son, Jadon, hands me a picture with scribbles outside the lines, I praise the beauty of his masterpiece and affirm his efforts. In the same way, when others share their alternative spiritual experiences, I realize that they are revealing the expression from which they as an individual artist draw their theological perspective. They may be diverse and often untrue impressions, but they reflect the personal and intellectual turmoil in each of their souls. I am not suggesting that we condone their portrayal but that we validate their personal illustration as a representation of seeking God.

In the past, community functioned by handing someone a piece of paper with boxes and lines. People were required to stay within those lines, using the same colors, expressing uniformity. Today, we need to hand people blank pieces of paper—no lines—and give them the freedom to be abstract and colorful. Only then can we offer to take their unique representation and add strokes of truth to point to greater definition.

Aligning with the undercurrent of this cultural tide forces us to take an alternative approach to ministry—which means changing a number of church practices.

Informational to Experiential

Within modernism, people discovered truth through the authority and power of reason—hence it is called the "Age of Reason." Modernism taught that the rational mind has the power to dissect, analyze, and grasp truth and to draw objective conclusions about reality.

Postmodernity, on the other hand, values multiple subjective truths gained through personal experiences. Many people may still value reason, but only if it is consistent with their experience. We've come to discover that information by itself leads to intellectualism, which doesn't necessarily lead to life change. Many postmoderns don't want merely to learn about God; they want to taste, feel, hear, and embrace their spirituality in holistic, tangible ways.

Aligning our missional strategy with this shift requires us to offer people the opportunity to engage with God's revelation in creative ways. Doing so will influence the way we arrange our communications, worship services, outreach, gatherings, small groups, leadership training, and process for discipleship.

Seclusion to Inclusion

Out of the Enlightenment came a common mantra voiced by many modernists that had to do with *the power of the individual*. They embraced the autonomous individualism of human existence. The freedom to make any choice was regarded as the ideal of this self-centered dogma—a freedom for people to do as they pleased and be what they pleased, without the intervention of others. However, the illusion was shattered as people began to realize that personal choice left up to the individual can result in choices that hinder personal freedom.

Now a new mantra of *social connectivity* champions the cause of individuals who wish to emerge from their lonely, fractured lives and pursue community. Meaningful, authentic relationships have always been a part of God's intent for humanity. Aligning our missional strategy has always demanded that we offer people the opportunity to engage in these meaningful, authentic relationships. Community must be the relational thread that influences their values.

Systems to Metaphor

Modernity preferred a systems-based language. Modernist education focused more on the ability to organize, analyze, and label beliefs and knowledge, placing them within systematic boxes. This reductionist approach allowed limited room for the use of story or metaphor. The mystery within such narratives was regarded as illogical and unreasonable. Rationalism was about teaching people what they needed to know. Postmoderns, on the other hand resonate with story and metaphor in the heart of their spirituality. Today's image- and icon-driven culture provides meaning and understanding to the world they live in.

Aligning our missional strategy with this shift requires us to communicate through the mediums of image and story. Every aspect of our process must have a narrative component, even as Jesus used illustrative parables to communicate truths of the kingdom.

Trust to Transfer

Modernism believed that humanity could trust in empirical data as its primary source of truth. Concrete data presented itself in convincing demonstrations, claiming to offer dependable, trustworthy conclusions. But postmoderns began growing skeptical when it became clear that many of the conclusions drawn are based on biased media networks or deceptive corporations who are simply marketing their products or services to consumers.

This leads to the Energizer versus Duracell question. Both claim to have data proving that their product is superior to the other. Consumers grow increasingly skeptical as to which claim is more believable. Postmoderns mistrust anyone who claims to have a corner on the truth. Sales pitches, slick marketing, and pithy slogans still have some influence on them. However, today the greater source of trust and transfer of truth can be found in relationships.

Aligning our missional strategy with this shift requires us to create space for people who aren't ready to believe or trust until they belong. A strategy that enables postmoderns to connect relationally is vital to transferring spiritual truths.

Uniformity to Diversity

Modernism struggled to control people's expression of spirituality by creating a one-way approach—individuals were taught one way to be, dress, speak, think, and create as Christians.

Today, postmoderns seek new ways to express their spirituality that break away from the stereotypical molds. They still value unity and seek to complement and inspire each other through their diversity. They understand there are many different ways of being a Christian, but they can still find ways of melding together in a cohesive, unified spiritual journey.

Aligning our missional strategy with this shift requires us to provide breathing space for individuals to discover and experiment. We must have a strategy that values unity amongst diversity.

Artificial to Organic

Within modernism, the expectation was that people would fall in line with a system of religion. Everyone presumed you would play your part in programmatic structures that outlined what was expected of you. For instance, when I was growing up in the church, all good Christian boys and girls were expected to go to church, attend the weekly prayer meeting, say a prayer before you eat, and wear your Sunday best. It didn't matter what was taking place inside as long you played your part. The focus was on behavior instead of authenticity.

Hierarchical structures of modernity limited the organic expression of individuality. The vertical chain of command suppressed and controlled individual behavior because it was seen as a threat to those higher up on the ladder. Postmoderns prefer the value of horizontal relational networks. These associations give birth to organic ventures and risky endeavors.

Aligning our missional strategy with this shift requires us to remove the threatened disposition of control and foster environments that inspire organic expressions in response to God's revelation. Refusing to attend a weekly prayer meeting doesn't imply that a person doesn't value prayer. In fact, he or she may have calloused knees and aspire to a unique experimentation of corporate prayer. Rather than being threatened by someone's "meeting" absence, we must create a strategy that guides, nourishes, and cultivates without having his or her expression completely refined or perfected. Authentic expression overshadows contrived behavior.

Then to Now

The redemptive mission of God hinges on a beautiful, mysterious story of salvation. Yet too often we give a narrow definition of salvation. We reduce it to something that's about sin and death only. Growing up in the church, I was always told that we need to believe in Jesus so that our sins can be forgiven and we can go to heaven when we die. This is true, but it's only part of the significance of salvation.

Eternal life is about so much more than a chronological or geographical destination. It is a holistic way of expressing a Christocentric quality of life passed on to us by the Spirit of God. Salvation is a window into the mystery and majesty of God. In our modernistic efforts to resolve every mystery, we have forgotten the necessity of the mystery. True, this window allows us to stand and gaze, giving us our approval for the afterlife, but it also allows us to engage in the daily, hourly, second-by-second mystery of our lives, metamorphosing into the image of the One who created us. It's in this ever-present mystery that our lives become a mirror reflecting back through the window the glory of our Savior. Postmoderns seek to experience the kingdom of God today, not just when they die.

Aligning ourselves with this shift requires us to communicate the salvation of God as something that can be experienced in people's lives right now, not just in the future.

Aligning with the Culture at Grace Chapel

Within Grace Chapel's strategic process of moving people from the park to the coffee shop to the living room, we seek to embrace every aspect of these cultural shifts of the postmodern epoch. Our desire is to see these new paradigms exhibited and expressed in the context of relational community. Each environment affirms the story line and plot of coexistence in pursuit of spiritual discovery and completion. Having an organic, relational strategy immerses our church in the cultural context of the postmodern mind.

Consider these thoughts of the late evangelical theologian Stanley Grenz in *A Primer on Postmodernism*:

> The conviction that each person is embedded in a particular human community leads to a corporate understanding of truth. Postmoderns believe that not only our specific beliefs but also our understanding of truth itself is rooted in the community in which we participate. They reject the Enlightenment quest for universal, supracultural, timeless truth in favor of searching out truth as the expression of a specific community.[5]

Assisting our current culture in the pursuit and discovery of redemptive truth happens as we engage in the communal construct. In the same way that Jesus bridges the gap between death and life, the church is to bridge the gap between truth and untruth as it engages relationally. Beliefs can become more strongly embraced as the church learns to connect those in our culture with those in our community of faith. This is faith in real life. This is the alignment of Grace Chapel's strategy to move people "from community to community."

Aligning with Leaders

All too often, churches have movement, yet everyone is moving in different directions with different goals, agendas, and expectations. As a result, churches sometimes take a shotgun approach to ministry in hopes of pleasing everyone—which in turn leads to confusion, politics, and, ultimately, stagnation. In churches without clear alignment, leaders compete rather than complement. Lack of clarity prevents them from aligning others with the process and creates confusion about the church's direction. And when this direction is ambiguous, people inevitably create their own.

Leaders are meant to influence others, to point them in a certain direction. It is necessary to create a simple and clear strategy to align all ministries to work in harmony with each other. They need to communicate the process in a way that everyone can comprehend. When alignment exists, various ministry leaders contribute in ways that demonstrate synergy with the whole team. The result is that the church is centered on a vision and strategy from the top down.

Aligning leaders around a strategic process means that they embrace and own it at the core of their responsibility. As they own the process, they align with it by weaving every goal, plan, and program into it. As Thom Rainer and Eric Geiger state in *Simple Church*,

> For the simple process to become a part of the culture of the church, it first must be woven into the leadership culture. The discussion must begin with the leadership of the

church. The simple process must become a part of their vocabulary. It must roll off their tongues with ease. It must make its way into the hallway discussions, lunches with key leaders, and the meetings.[6]

This fosters a leadership culture that lives, breathes, and models alignment with a single strategic process. As a result, the larger community of faith takes its cues from the leadership and joins in with full buy-in. The difference between leading a church and leading a movement is the ability to align leaders around a strategic process in such a way that others begin to passionately align themselves with it too.

Once alignment happens among the leaders, it is vital to articulate the process on a regular basis. Sharing through sermons, videos, stories, Internet communications, and any other means can help keep the process in front of your church. People need to be reminded of the process and affirmed for living it out. Nothing is more rewarding than hearing people begin to use the vocabulary of the process in their everyday conversations.

Every year, Grace Chapel starts a new season of ministry by gathering together all of our leaders to review our strategic process and identify how each of us can play a part in it. We also have weekly staff meetings that are more like family time with our fellow teammates.

But about a year ago, we decided to change what our meetings would look like. We shifted our focus from solving ministry objectives to celebrating stories of life change. Now it's a one-hour community gathering centered on highlighting what we see God doing in our church. The expectation is that each staff member will come prepared to share stories of that work. It's also a time for bragging about each other and how we see God using one another in our ministries. Deep inside, I think we all love it when someone else talks about us. It feeds something in each of us who want to know that God is using us in great ways.

These meetings have brought us together in a remarkable way. Our stories ground us in what we are all about, enabling staff members to respond well when someone asks, "How do you see God moving in your church?" Through this time of sharing, our perspectives are broadened to see the amazing things that are taking place among us. These weekly meetings help align us with our strategy by keeping us accountable to what we're all about.

Churches are thrust into movement when they experience alignment among their calling, purpose, mission, culture, leadership, people, and strategic process. Alignment functions like a powerful energy source. It can be dangerous and fierce, depending on how it's used. Once you begin to experience alignment, the big question is, Now where do we go and what do we do with it?

In response, it's time to take faith into real life by moving into the culture—that is, the "park" environment.

Part 2

the park

4

hermaphrodites and other lovable people

Finding Hubs

It was 6:00 a.m. when I started the V-8 engine of my Dodge Ram pickup. I was on my way to a special meeting. I had no reason to be anxious, but for some reason this particular meeting had my stomach rolling like a kid who had just scarfed down an entire box of Captain Crunch and chased it with a box of Twinkies.

The meeting I was driving to would set a precedent for our church's role in the community. A few weeks earlier, I had contacted several local groups that worked directly with impoverished individuals and families. I spoke to school counselors and principals, community center leaders, and people who worked at the local food bank because they were witnessing the effects of poverty and hunger every day. My hope was to get them around a table and initiate a conversation about partnering to address these issues in our community. So I invited them to breakfast at a local restaurant.

To my surprise, everyone accepted the invitation. As I drove, all sorts of thoughts, concerns, and questions raced through my mind. I had no idea how the meeting would go. Was the fact that I'm a pastor going to be a turnoff? Would they be interested in working with a church, or would they want nothing to do with a bunch of "Jesus people"? Over the years, we had accumulated a bit of social capital with these organizations; now I was spending it all on this one appointment. I was hoping they would let me into their circle of trust.

As I crossed the I–5 bridge over the Willamette River it dawned on me: This morning could turn out to see the crossing of a more significant metaphorical bridge—one that joined church and culture. I pulled into the parking lot of the Garlic Onion Ristorante, said a quick prayer for God's favor, and got out of my truck. Zach, a school counselor, was already waiting inside. One by one, each person I had invited walked through the restaurant doors.

After we took our seats, I simply acknowledged that I was excited to see them. And then I bribed them: "Breakfast is on Grace Chapel, so please order what you like." Most went for the breakfast buffet, making me feel right at home. It brought me back to the Baptist potluck days of my childhood—minus all the pushing and shoving in line.

A few moments passed, and as everyone began to eat, I opened the conversation. "On behalf of our church, I just want to thank you for all you're doing for the poor in our community." I felt some gratitude was long overdue. "The reason I wanted us to get together is so we can start a dialogue about the needs in our community and what our church can do to help."

There. It was out there now. My agenda.

The table lit up with ideas as each person shared his or her perspective. The most interesting comment came from a woman named Sandi who was sitting to my left. Sandi was the chairperson on the board of the local food bank. She had a full-time job as a director of city development. In other words, Sandi was an important person in our city who had influence over such things as building permits. My first impression of Sandi was that of a strict librarian with a monochromatic personality—a petite, middle-aged woman with short hair, traditional glasses, and conservative attire. I had picked up from an earlier conversation that she was not a Christian or a churchgoer.

As Sandi began to speak, she said something so profound that it seemed to be prophetic. "What our city needs is a heart—a place where people know they can go to find help, compassion, and care." It's really not that profound that she would recognize that people need to experience compassion and care. It *does* seem profound that she would ask our church to be the center for finding it.

She was right! Her statement fired me up like a shot of adrenalin.

Her comment was followed by one from a school counselor named Katie. Looking right at me, she said, "You guys could be the heart of our city. You are like our Oprah."

I took her comment as a compliment, not as a suggestion that our church ought to resemble a talk show. With resounding unity, these influential community leaders proposed that our church take the lead in rallying our city to address the needs of our community. What started out as a simple question had become a platform of opportunity to influence an entire city.

I could not help but ask myself, What if the church emerged as the heart of a city? The epicenter of compassion and care? For years it had been my dream to help build a hybrid church/ community center. A church that would serve as a cultural hub. Instead of erecting a building for our own needs and desires, I have always imagined a place that serves as a career center, a medical clinic, a counseling practice, a recreational facility, a teen center, a food bank, a creative arts theatre, and a business conference space.

As the breakfast meeting was coming to a close, Sandi asked all sorts of questions about our church. "Are you guys a part of a large denomination?" she inquired.

"No, we're just a single independent church."

"What else do you do at your church?"

"Several things locally, but we also built a hospital in Nicaragua and an orphanage in Rwanda." I said.

Sandi was so moved by what she heard that tears began to form in her eyes. Clearly, this had turned out to be a divine appointment—a great foundation to build on.

The church is in danger of becoming more and more isolated. Without its own relational strategy to engage the world, churches fade into seclusion and become strangers to their communities. The church must rediscover its incarnational role and start building bridges. We must connect.

Reconnecting the church with its community is a driving focus of Grace Chapel's "park" environment. Within each community there are natural hubs of influence—relational frameworks that can increase the social exposure of the church. These hubs (for example, local schools, civic organizations, and other groups) provide unique opportunities to get outside our church walls and converge on common ground.

Every church can find its unique place of influence among their natural community hubs. Incarnating in these places will inspire us to see culture in a new way.

Chasm of Confusion

Your church is probably doing amazing things, yet those in the surrounding community often have no idea what you are achieving.

It's easy for us to withdraw from culture rather than see ourselves as an integral part of it. Sometimes we employ this tactic to deal with our fear of the world. Let's be honest. Some things in this world leave us feeling scared, confused, and troubled. The voices of terror within cry out to dwell in a secure place. As a result, we may build walls of safety, otherwise known as "the Christian subculture." But there is an alternative view of separation in the Bible that can inspire us to break free from the coziness of the Christian subculture.

Biblical separation is known as *sanctification*—a word that refers to "the act or process of making something (or someone) holy or set apart." *Sanctification* is translated from the Greek word *hagiasmos* ("purification"), from the root *hagios* ("holy" or "sacred").

Sanctification has everything to do with position, process, and purpose. Sanctification is an act of God by which he "sets apart" a person, place, or object. When sanctified, we are in *position*—set apart and declared as holy. We are also sanctified in *purpose*—being set apart by God for a specific divine intention. Lastly, we are sanctified in *process*—from salvation as we begin the progression of being conformed to the image of Jesus Christ.

Being set apart as holy suggests something that is the opposite of sinful. Often we draw the conclusion that culture is sinful; therefore, to be holy we must separate ourselves from it. The irony is that when the church separates itself from culture, it forces people outside the church to view the bride of Christ from a distance. This distance becomes a chasm of confusion, leading others to draw incorrect conclusions about Christ based on misunderstandings.

It was never God's intention to take Christians out of culture. It has always been his objective to change culture through

Christians. Jesus prays to the Father, "My prayer is *not that you take them out* of the world but that you protect them from the evil one" (John 17:15, emphasis added). The church is a masterpiece of divine artistry, an exquisite portrait of broken lives transformed into a new mosaic. Its radiance should reach into the furthest expressions of humanity.

Pop Culture

The word *culture* has many different meanings. For some, it refers to an appreciation of good literature, music, art, and food. For anthropologists and other behavioral scientists, however, culture encompasses the full range of learned human behavior.

The term was first used this way by the English anthropologist Edward B. Tylor in his book *Primitive Culture*, published in 1871. Tylor wrote that culture is "that complex whole which includes knowledge, belief, art, law, morals, custom, and any other capabilities and habits acquired by man as a member of society."[7]

I would label *culture* as "the collective expression of worldviews." A worldview is the grid by which we interpret life's most puzzling questions. It serves as a lens for thinking and believing. A worldview is an anthology of beliefs about God, truth, reality, the world, humanity, history, death, knowledge, and values. Our worldview shapes how we evaluate, make decisions, and create a sense of meaning for our lives. Culture, then, becomes the expression of worldviews through art, science, education, recreation, law, and customs.

Every human being—regardless of what we think of him or her—bears the image of God. This intrinsic spirituality of humanity is reflected in culture. Culture tells us everything we need to know about the positive and negative ways in which people respond to God's revelation. There is much expressed in culture that represents exactly how God wants his image bearers to respond to him. Sadly, there is also much in culture that grieves the heart of God.

Instead of vacating culture, though, we should validate the good in culture and offer illumination to that which is dark.

Consider Paul's approach as he engaged the Greek culture of Athens: "While Paul was waiting for [Silas and Timothy] in Athens, he was greatly distressed to see that the city was full of idols" (Acts 17:16).

Why do you think Paul was distressed over their idols? Was he offended by the iconic statues, or was he saddened because they did not know the one and only living God? I love the fact that he did not picket these idols with a cardboard sign, yelling, "God hates idols." He could have stood from a distance and lobbed pithy religious grenades. Instead, he inserted himself into society: "So he reasoned in the synagogue with both Jews and God-fearing Greeks, as well as in the marketplace day by day with those who happened to be there" (Acts 17:17).

Notice how Paul expanded his influence from the synagogues into the marketplace. I can't see Paul standing on a street corner in the ancient equivalent of Times Square, wearing a T-shirt that reads, "Jesus is God with skin on." As Paul engaged the culture of Athens, a wider conversation began:

> A group of Epicurean and Stoic philosophers began to debate with him. Some of them asked, "What is this babbler trying to say?" Others remarked, "He seems to be advocating foreign gods." They said this because Paul was preaching the good news about Jesus and the resurrection.
>
> ACTS 17:18

Ironically, the approach of these Epicureans and Stoics had much in common with the mind-set of many modern

Americans. Epicureans believed that the greatest good was to seek modest pleasures in order to attain a state of tranquility and freedom from fear; one's own pleasure, rather than service to God, was the greatest good. Stoicism was the most popular self-help philosophy of its day. It held to the notion that "virtue" is the highest goal and that humanity can rise above any circumstance by one's outlook on life. Everything really good or bad in one's life depended only on one's self. Essentially, Paul was sparring in an intellectual joust between Howard Stern and Dr. Phil. Amazingly, Paul earned the opportunity to be heard, as shown in the next verses:

> Then they took him and brought him to a meeting of the Areopagus, where they said to him, "May we know what this new teaching is that you are presenting? You are bringing some strange ideas to our ears, and we would like to know what they mean." (All the Athenians and the foreigners who lived there spent their time doing nothing but talking about and listening to the latest ideas.)
>
> ACTS 17:19–21

Doing nothing but talking and listening to the latest ideas? Sounds like pop culture to me. Pop culture reveals its expression in the mass circulation of current trends and ideas. Paul found himself being invited into one of the greatest circles of influence within the popular culture of his day. His divine appointment gave him a platform to dialogue with these cultural leaders:

> Paul then stood up in the meeting of the Areopagus and said: "People of Athens! I see that in every way you are very religious. For as I walked around and looked carefully at your objects of worship, I even found an altar with this

inscription: TO AN UNKNOWN GOD. So you are ignorant of the very thing you worship—and this is what I am going to proclaim to you."

ACTS 17:22–23

Taking full advantage of his platform, Paul affirmed their religious devotion and introduced his homily by referencing a god they worshiped but were ignorant of. He pointed out that he had "looked carefully" at their objects of worship. He was deliberate in studying their cultural expressions—the religious manifestations of their worldview. Paul's commitment to understand their culture gave him the opportunity to influence and illuminate in a relevant way.

Engaging the culture in this way can unlock the mystery of your community's concept of spirituality.

Recently, I had a fascinating conversation with Bobby Gruenewald of LifeChurch.tv. Bobby is an innovative thinker with a passion to see the gospel infiltrate culture. LifeChurch.tv has a priority to seat themselves at the table of culture and participate in the significant discussions that are taking place there. So I decided to ask Bobby how he sees the church's engagement with culture.

"The church has historically been a part of shaping its culture," he began. "However, several years ago—decades ago—the church appeared to be almost absent from that conversation. Within the last couple of decades, the church has tried to catch up and mimic culture instead of creating it." He went on to say that it is our responsibility to figure out how to connect to culture.

In the same way in which Paul connected with those in culture by using the platform of a common spiritual exploration, the church must do anything, short of engaging in sin, to utilize the platform that culture offers us.

Hazards of Humanity

For many Christians, the word *culture* carries a scary association. Like a malevolent fog hovering in the chill of night. Or like
the effect of these lyrics from the song "Thriller," performed by
Michael Jackson: "It's close to midnight and something evil's
lurking in the dark.... You start to freeze as horror looks you
right between the eyes. You're paralyzed."[8]

One Saturday morning, I found myself paralyzed in response
to a conversation I had with someone in our community. Due to
budget cuts, a local elementary school could no longer afford the
upkeep of its campus. We offered to send volunteers to help the
school's staff deal with the overgrown weeds and thick, unruly
hedges. Armed with shovels, rakes, gloves, and trimmers, we
set out on our own version of *Extreme Makeover: Home Edition*.

Between endless wheelbarrow trips back and forth to the
bark pile, I was approached by one of the schoolteachers. From
the look in his eyes, it was clear he wanted to talk with me.
Either that, or I had just rolled over the new flowers they just
planted!

"So, tell me more about your church," he said as he rested
his arms on his shovel.

"What do you want to know?"

"What does your church think about homosexuals?"

Talk about your loaded question.

Standing there, frozen, I felt completely unprepared to
engage such a hot topic. I kept thinking of Jerry Seinfeld and
George Costanza saying over and over again, "Not that there's
anything wrong with that." It was unnerving. I did not know
what to say.

Eventually emerging from my petrified disposition, I
responded by saying the only thing I could think of. "Our

church does not make an issue out of it. Our goal is to introduce people to a relationship with God and then sort that out later."

How cliché!

Why did his question seem to threaten me? Was it because I thought his worldview might jeopardize my faith and challenge my theology? What a missed opportunity! I had resorted to a quick answer, hoping to escape the discomfort of the dialogue. Behind his question was a story. I wish I had taken the time to ask him to tell me more, and to listen.

From that moment, I knew I had been sheltered. My desire to deflect the difficult issues of my culture had suppressed my ability to connect with others.

It is a dangerous risk to be in the world but not of it. It cost Jesus his life—and it may well cost us ours. Leading a movement means you have to embrace the hazards of humanity in ways that may jeopardize self-preservation.

By refusing to embrace this risk, however, we may risk a lot more. We may become unable to recognize the unmistakable reality of Christ manifesting himself within our communities. This was the case with the Gnostics, who were the subject of John's letters to the church. Gnosticism believed that God was far too pure to have anything to do with the material universe, which was considered evil. Since Gnosticism taught that all matter is evil, it denied the incarnation of God's Son. Hence John's statement: "This is how you can recognize the Spirit of God: Every spirit that acknowledges that Jesus Christ has come in the flesh is from God, but every spirit that does not acknowledge Jesus is not from God" (1 John 4:2–3).

Gnostics did not acknowledge or identify the revelation of God through Christ within their own culture. In a similar fashion, our presupposition that culture is evil may keep us from recognizing the presence of God in our culture.

Efforts to reach culture from a distance often adopt an attractional strategy rather than an incarnational strategy. An attractional strategy assumes that we know the questions people are asking, and so it seeks to provide answers to these questions. An incarnational strategy does not assume it automatically knows what questions people are asking; instead, it discovers the questions by engaging culture and seeks to answer these questions in ways to which the culture can relate.

It is possible that we may actually think our style of worship, casual dress, new technology, and informal sermons make us relevant to culture. This is the sad illusion that so many churches live and die by. I believe that relevance happens when the ultimate answer, Jesus Christ, is expressed through a church that intersects with the world he created.

Several years ago, I was invited to a party held in a city park. A young woman from our church, Shauna, had approached me one Sunday after church and said, "I'm hosting this party for all of my apartment building neighbors next week in the park, and I think it would be a great opportunity for you to meet some people in our community."

The following Sunday, I arrived at the park around 5:00 p.m. I noticed a large gathering underneath one of the large shelters. As I approached the crowd, I quickly noticed that this was a hodgepodge of interesting individuals. I am an extrovert by nature — but this anomalous assortment of characters had my people skills working overtime. I made a few polite introductions and blended in with the pack.

Shauna found me. "Would you open in prayer and bless the food?" she asked with eagerness.

"You bet," I said with artificial enthusiasm.

In the short time I had been there, I'd already had a conversation with a Muslim woman. I was certain this crowd represented a melting pot of religious expression. By asking me to pray, Shauna was either calling me out or throwing me under the bus. A big part of me did not want to pray and reveal my secret identity of a pastor. (Besides, there was no phone booth nearby to change in.) Once people discover that you're a pastor, it has a tendency to repel the authenticity from conversation.

Reluctantly, I prayed a short prayer.

Immediately afterward, I felt a tap on my shoulder. As I turned around I observed a tall, middle-aged man towering over me. He introduced himself as Jim.*

"You're a pastor?"

"Yes."

He was nervous. "Can I talk to you about something?" he whispered. I noticed the anxious tone in his voice.

"I've visited a lot of churches over the past few years, but I haven't been able to find one that would accept me."

"I am sorry to hear that. What made it hard for you to connect?"

"I am a hermaphrodite. I was born with both male and female genitalia." Jim went on to make his point by showing his driver's license, which declared him as "male/female."

He amplified on his dilemma. "My whole life I've struggled to fit in, especially at church. I've gone back and forth, taking hormone supplements, struggling to resolve who I am."

I could only imagine the unrest of his soul.

Then Jim revealed the issue that plagued him at his very core. "I don't think God accepts me because of what I am."

Jim's perception of God was shaped by the shame and the rejection he felt at church. Putting my hand on Jim's shoulder to convey acceptance, I said, "Jim, not only does God love you,

---

*Names have been changed throughout to protect privacy.

but he understands every hurt and thought of rejection you've experienced."

Immediately there was a change in Jim's demeanor from dishonor to increased dignity. I never saw Jim again, but my last impression of him was something that I entrusted God to take into eternity. I knew I would take it into mine.

How often do we form our views and our strategies for reaching culture within a vacuum? When we live in a vacuum, we make assumptions about what the people in our community think, feel, question, and hurt about—rather than simply engaging with people.

Our concern should not be to make God relevant. He is and always will be. Our concern is to connect the relevance of God to the culture we live in without making assumptions. This is called "contextualizing the gospel." If we hope to reach the culture, we need a contextualized approach that understands and uses the languages and concepts of those we are engaging.

Pastor and author Tim Keller articulates this tension in an essay titled "Ministry in the New Global Culture of Major City Centers." He writes, "To reach a new culture, the gospel must enter, challenge, and re-tell the story of the new culture."[9]

While teaching a class at Multnomah Bible College called "Worldviews," I required every student to undertake a semester-long cultural immersion project called "ethnography"—the study of human culture. This project involved participating in people's lives for an extended period of time, watching what happens, listening to what is said, and asking questions. It forces us to change our posture toward those in culture and make the effort to understand their hearts, struggles, questions, and fears. It means putting down the picket signs, getting off our soapboxes, and crossing the barriers of our own pride. Instead of raising banners declaring God's anger toward gays, why not use the five dollars' worth of paint and cardboard to listen to some-one's story over a cup of coffee? This is incarnational living.

Incarnational living is about downward mobility. To live in the shadow of the cross is to embark in the challenge of contin-ual descent. Along the journey, we're invited to embrace a life of selflessness—of living for the sake of others. The incarnation of Jesus Christ was more than heaven living on earth. During his life, Jesus continued the descent from heaven to earth, from earth to the margins, and from the margins to the cross.

Incarnational living promotes a spirituality that takes on a persona of being lowered so that others may be lifted. Living incarnationally is about more than where we buy our grocer-ies or sip our lattes. It's the life we model where we buy our groceries and sip our lattes. It demands a willingness to make a continual effort to understand the marginalized and deprived. It values association with the "least of these" (Matthew 25:40) over personal advancement.

I think of a young single mom who approached me after church one day. She was accompanied by a somewhat disheveled man. My hand grasped his as she introduced us. He was a home-less man whom she had befriended during one of her weekly vis-its to the street community. Frequently she gathers clothes, food, blankets, and water and commutes to a nearby area populated by homeless dwellers. But she doesn't run a ministry organization. What's even more amazing is that she's a single mom with serious and painful health issues. But this is her way of living incarna-tionally—of lowering herself so others may be lifted up.

Cultural Hubs

The infrastructure of every community is made up of several components: commerce, the arts, technology, entertainment, education, government, benevolence, and recreation. These components operate simultaneously as they synchronize within the daily lives of the people. Each has its own channels of influence that drive persuasion within society. Being a cultural architect, or one who harmonizes the strategy to fit his or her culture, is to dissect these hubs with a goal of finding entry points. It's amazing to think of how much influence a church can have in its community simply by engaging with these entry points.

As I began the process of dissecting the cultural hubs present within the community at Grace Chapel, it became clear that our local public schools were a significant nucleus of relational influence. I decided to make a cold call to each of the four public school principals in our area. My first call was to a middle school principal named Barb.

I introduced myself as a pastor at Grace Chapel.

"What can I do for you?" she asked.

"I was hoping I could meet with you to discuss a service project that our church would like to do for your campus."

"Sure. I have an opening next week."

One after the other, each area principal agreed to meet. Sitting in their offices reminded me of those childhood feelings of anxiety caused by my frequent visits to the principal's office. I shared my church's desire to start something called the "All-City Cleanup." We wanted to show up at their schools on a Saturday morning to help renew their campuses. I asked each principal to share his or her list of projects that had been neglected and needed immediate attention. This one question gave me the opportunity to spend quality time with them surveying their campuses.

At Grace Chapel, we want all of our small groups to be missional communities. We cast the vision to see what kind of impact we could have if all of our groups rallied together for a single project.

The plan was to have all of the groups arrive at the high school at noon on Saturday. Living in Portland pretty much guarantees lousy weather, especially in April. That morning, I drove to the school as raindrops assaulted the windshield of my truck. Convinced that the torrential buckets of rain would bring this event to an untimely end, I pleaded for God to turn the water off. Not only did he *not* stop the rain; by the time everyone arrived, he decided to show off by making it rain sideways (that's wind plus rain). To my complete and bewildered amazement, hundreds of people began showing up, and for three hours everyone labored while getting drenched by the miserable weather.

Spirits were high, and, despite the weather, we experienced a powerful bonding. People remarked that it was a highlight for them and their families to be part of a church that ventured outside its own walls. In the end, our efforts left the schools transformed and immaculate.

A few months had passed when Andy, the principal of the high school, called. "Mike, I'm just calling to say thanks for all that your church did to renovate our campus."

"It was a great day for us," I said. "Thanks for letting us do it."

"There is something else I want to ask you," he said. "We have a school board meeting coming up, and we would like to present your church with a certificate of appreciation. Would you be there to receive it?"

Completely overwhelmed by surprise, I said, "Absolutely."

"And there is something else," he continued. "Would you be able to take a few minutes to speak to the board and the audience about why your church did this project?"

I agreed, but I nearly fell out of my chair. This was crazy! We live in one of the most liberal, unchurched states in the country—and the public school board wanted me to speak about what motivates our church.

I liked Andy, and I was pretty sure he was not a believer. As he made his opening statements to the school board, Andy reflected on what impacted him the most: "Seeing hundreds of volunteers show up in such horrible weather demonstrated to me their heart to reach out to our schools. We are very grateful to have a church like this in our community."

That moment will forever be captured in my mind.

This platform became an opportunity to have influence within the school district. The following year, we decided to build on that platform, now that trust had been established. Once more we offered to provide volunteers for a similar project. This time, word spread through the school's natural hubs of influence, affirming our role in the community. PTA meetings, faculty meetings, newsletters, local newspapers, and school marquees displayed their appreciation for what we were doing. The influence they carried in their own relational networks multiplied, carrying the message more effectively than anything we could have done by ourselves.

This was only the beginning of our efforts to tap into our community's relational framework. Another hub of influence we've partnered with is our local community center. Over the past year, our children's community director, Angie Rettman, sensed that there needed to be another evolution of outreach to her ministry. Instead of putting the resources and volunteer efforts into another successful Vacation Bible School, she decided to take VBS off the table and replace it with something more effective at engaging the community. She met with Brian, who oversees the youth programs at the local community center, to ask about and listen to his needs.

Brian was thoroughly impressed by her gesture of concern and care for the program's needs.

Brian went on to explain that every summer they organize an "Art in the Park" weekly program, designed to help families experience togetherness and relational well-being. The program has been such a success that the turnout has left the community center overwhelmed, unstaffed, and no longer capable of managing it. As Brian explained to Angie the need for someone to help take ownership of "Art in the Park," it was no surprise that he was impressed by her sincerity. (It's exactly what Angie had hoped would happen.) Now, in partnership with the community center, our church will transfer our VBS resources and volunteer efforts into helping to lead our community's "Art in the Park" program.

You might think a significant amount of people would have been upset that we weren't offering VBS that year. On the contrary, the decision was remarkably affirmed. As I sat in Angie's office that week, celebrating her new direction in partnering with one of our cultural hubs, we recognized that this particular "Art in the Park" event was literally taking place in our local parks. Again it affirmed our metaphor of the "park" environment.

Another hub of influence we've connected to is our local Chamber of Commerce. Every city has one. Last Christmas, a woman in our church approached me with an idea.

Anne is the manager of a local bank. She is also the point person for organizing an annual Christmas fund-raising banquet on behalf of the Chamber of Commerce. Being a huge fan of the videos we produce at our church, she proposed an idea. "This year's theme for the Chamber is 'capturing the spirit of Christmas,'" she explained. "Would Grace Chapel consider producing a video to be featured at the event?"

I was intrigued. "Sounds good. What would it look like?"

With an energized look in her eyes, she answered, "We want to do interviews with several business owners sharing their thoughts on the spirit of Christmas."

Our video producer and I traveled throughout the city, visiting business owners and filming their candid reflections. The interviews gave us access to several influential members of our community. The following week, we were invited to attend the fund-raising banquet as special guests. The room was overflowing with hundreds of people. The video was well received, and as the program came to a close, frequent gestures of appreciation were expressed. Word spread throughout the business community, further expanding our platform as their natural hub of influence increased ours.

Our churches are filled with people like Anne—people who serve in these hubs of influence. I also think of Scott and Brad, who are good friends who attend our church. Both hold key positions of influence within our city's political infrastructure. Some of my favorite conversations have featured brainstorming about how to leverage their influence in partnership with our church to make a significant impact on our community.

Leaders can and should leverage the influence of the people in our churches. People thrive on the opportunity to help the church have influence within its part of the cultural framework. Instead of being preoccupied with ourselves, the shared values within these cultural hubs provide access for us to have common ground. It's what brings us to the table together.

At Grace Chapel, we are just beginning to see the potential of these strategic partnerships between those sitting in the chairs of our church and the networks they belong to.

One afternoon, as I was walking down the sidewalk, a woman emerged from her house.

"You're a pastor at that church that does all those things in the community, right?" she asked.

I answered cautiously, "Yes."

"I just want you to know how much we value having you as a part of our community."

It is responses such as this one that provide the payoff to the investment and a reminder of what God is doing through our "park" environment.

LifeChurch.tv, where Bobby Gruenewald serves in ministry, understands that technology is a key aspect of culture and represents yet another substantial hub of influence. Recently, Life-Church.tv launched YouVersion, an online virtual community centered on Scripture. YouVersion has become one of the top fifty apps for the iPhone, with 225,000 people downloading it in the first month alone.

When I asked Bobby how he was able to be an influence within the technological hub, he said, "We try to be intentional about engaging in the spheres of influence. That means everything from advising start-up businesses to sitting on boards to attending technology conferences. We participate in discussions where the church is a completely foreign concept in those discussions, in fact, sometimes even is held in contempt. But for me, that's a place where we can be part of the discussion and gain understanding about what new things are out there that we can embrace or be a part of developing that can impact the world."

Throughout this journey, I've come to understand that three things are critical to establishing relationships within the natural hubs of influence. I call them the "3Cs" of connecting with culture: contact, consistency, and connection. *Contact* represents the initial stage and hints at the importance of being intentional about associating with others. Once the initial contact has been made—perhaps through a service project or partnership—it is essential to demonstrate consistency. *Consistency* builds trust and opens dialogue for deeper relationships. The result of consistent contact is relational *connection*, which leads to increased platforms for greater influence within our cultural networks.

The goal for these 3Cs is the experience of that unique and powerful redemptive process of seeing a life changed through the revealing of Christ in someone's life. Our "park" environment includes any service project, community event, strategic partnership, or small group outreach that accomplishes the evolution of the 3Cs.

Concealed within the church is the beautiful bride of Christ. The bride stands before all to be deemed as either a presentation of splendor or a spectacle of self-indulgence. I believe that the unblemished veil is lifted in full disclosure as we seek the opportunity to live our faith courageously in the real-life arenas that revolve around us every day. And maybe, there to be discovered, is another hermaphrodite waiting for you to affirm their seat at the table.

5

eggsactly wrong

Marketing with a Twist

I was tired after a long day of two worship services followed by two afternoon meetings. The only thing I wanted to do when I got home was veg in front of the TV. Crawling out of the vehicle and making my weary way to the front door, I heard a voice shout from across the street.

"Hey, Mike!"

Part of me wanted to pretend I hadn't heard anything, but I glanced over my shoulder to see who was addressing me. It was my neighbor from across the street. Being an extrovert and a pastor, I'm usually geared up to dive into relational conversations, but there are also those moments (often) when I feel so overwhelmed by people that all I want to do is check out. It's usually after a season of ministry overdose that I begin to reveal the Mr. Hyde inside of me. This happened to be one of those sinister transforming moments. But even in this frame of mind, I could still sense the Holy Spirit nudging me to walk across the street and talk with my neighbor.

"Hey, what's up?" I shouted back as I sauntered diagonally across the street.

Bill was born and raised in Hawaii. His wife and three

teenage daughters moved into our neighborhood a year earlier. His career as a truck driver, his full-body tattoos, ferocious pit bull, and colorful vocabulary pretty much stereotype him as one gnarly dude. At least he intimidated the heck out of me! He makes Chuck Norris look like Cinderella in an evening dress.

As soon as the rubber of my sneakers converged with his driveway, he extended an offer for a cold one. It was his gesture of friendship.

Sip after sip and through all the small talk, I tried to force back the image of a pretentious, professional "holy man." Then he caught me off guard with some disheartening news. "My sister died today."

Stunned by his willingness to share so candidly with me, I expressed my sympathy.

Bill's eyes began to water. "Bro, could you pray for me?"

Humbled by his brokenness and even more captivated by the meek alteration of his brusque ego, I placed my arm around him and uttered a few words in prayer. The end of my prayer was greeted by a flood of emotion, as Bill embraced me, shedding tears on my shoulder. It was an odd scene, and part of me wondered what our neighbors were thinking. There I was standing with the toughest guy in our suburban housing complex — in full embrace, his close-shaved, stubbly head nestled in my shoulder. A part of me couldn't help but think that people might start to wonder if I am playing for the wrong team.

After several minutes of unguarded sharing, Bill asked me a second remarkable question. "Can someone like me go to your church?"

"Absolutely. Anyone can come to our church," I insisted.

Somehow the answer, which seemed so obvious in my mind,

defied the weight of all the false perceptions of Churchianity he was carrying.

One way or another, his impression of church had led him to one of two possible conclusions: church attendance required a personal invitation, or no church would accept the likes of him.

A final round of handshakes and hugs, a few encouraging words—and then I proceeded on to my house.

My wife greeted me at the foyer of our home. "What was *that* all about?" she asked with a concerned look on her face.

After I filled her in, she responded immediately. "I think we need to do something to help them."

"I agree. What did you have in mind? I know they're planning on taking out a loan to purchase airline tickets to Hawaii."

Our nine-year-old daughter Mikiah was eavesdropping on our conversation and exclaimed, "We should help them pay for their tickets."

In those defining moments when your kids just seem to "get it," there is nothing you can do but affirm their childlike brilliance. As a child with the sympathetic heart of a mature Christ-follower, our daughter inspired me to live out the compassion of Jesus.

With crisp folded bills in my hand, I knocked on their door. The door cracked open, revealing Bill's face.

"Come on in, Mike," Bill said with a warm smile.

Standing in their foyer, I stretched out my hand to offer the money. "It's not much," I said, "but it will help get your family on the plane."

Round 2 of hugging and crying started all over again—this time with the added expression of kissing. (Yes, kissing—but not in a *Will & Grace* kind of way.) Honestly, I was uncomfortable having a grown man whom I barely knew exhibit such a personal display of affection, especially when it involved his hairy lips and my exposed cheek. (When I went home and told my wife about his reaction, she laughed and said it was good for me. I spent the rest of the night watching *Rambo*.) Amid the awkward squeezes and repetitive pecking, Bill motioned for his wife to come to the door. As he explained what had taken place, her eyes began to swell with tears, and she decided to join the hugfest.

Nothing tears down cynics' walls more tangibly than acts of compassion and kindness. The love that compelled Jesus to serve the "least of these" (Matthew 25:40) is the same radical love that makes the church irresistible today. The good news is that even those who may mistrust the church still value compassion. We tend to miss this amazing opportunity for connection when we focus our attention on what we're against rather than on what we are for.

It all comes down to marketing.

No Marketing

The reality is that advertising and marketing are inevitable. One way or another, you as a person and as a church are marketing something. If you think that resisting or boycotting the act of putting your church on display for others to examine is in some way nobler, less compromising, or more spiritual, you're not seeing the full imprint you're capable of making.

Take, for example, tips and ties—yes, neckties. My sister-in-law has worked as a waitress at several restaurants in the Portland area. Like many in this industry, she makes a good portion of her income from the tips left by customers. For a while, she worked at a restaurant located on the grounds of the Rose Garden, our city's premier sports arena. Each year the Rose Garden hosts a certain large Christian conference. (I won't mention which one, . . . ladies!) As her restaurant would fill up with conference attendees, she noticed a pattern. The tips from these Christian customers were considerably smaller than non-Christian customers—even borderline insulting. Of course the post-church Sunday crowds were no better. Her experience led her to conclude that Christians are cheap.

Here's another example. Every Sunday evening, as I drive past a church just down the street from my house, I take notice of the well-dressed men sporting neckties and suit coats. I am sure they are a great church, and I'm not judging the fact that they wear ties to church. I'm just pointing out the fact that people are observing us and our churches under the microscope, and whatever they notice—from tips to ties—advertises something about who we are to them, whether we admit it or not.

Unfortunately, the deck is already stacked against us. Consider the research done by David Kinnaman and Gabe Lyons in their book *UnChristian*. They cite six impressions that unchurched people have toward Christians: we are hypocritical, too focused on getting converts, antihomosexual, sheltered, too political, and judgmental. The authors note that "Christianity's image problem is not merely the perception of young outsiders. Those inside the church see it as well—especially Christians in their twenties and thirties."[10] Whether or not we believe these six perceptions accurately reflect reality, they are a result of what kind of brand Christians are marketing.

"No marketing" is an illusion. Every church markets something.

Church Marketing

Christmas and Easter are the two days when the unchurched are most likely to consider showing up at church. So every year, churches spend massive amounts on marketing, direct mail, postcards, newspaper ads, and local cable TV ads. So much energy is poured into creative efforts to make our churches attractive. We try to communicate that we are hip, relevant, contemporary, even convenient—in the hope that a clever post-card will inspire an unchurched person to seriously reconsider their habit of church abstinence. In fact, some church mailings invoke more repulsion than magnetism. My personal favorite was a piece inviting people to "Join Us for Easter EGGcite-ment!" On the reverse side:

Tear open gifts in Easter basket: 3 minutes.

Find hidden eggs: 30 minutes, if you're lucky.

Now what?

If you're finding there's not much left to your Easter but empty eggshells, join us for a little EGGcitement! Here you'll find welcoming people, great music, and a sermon that's challenging and relevant. Your kids will enjoy pint-sized activities, making new friends and even learning something new! It's EGGsactly what your family needs this Easter!

For years Grace Chapel invested thousands of dollars in this kind of marketing. Year after year, we would design mailers and barrage the entire community with information about our services, hoping it would somehow entice people to join us. We put all of our eggs in the one basket of glossy 3x5s.

Advertising and marketing are all about branding. And branding is about identity. So as we thought about our adver-tising and marketing, I began to ask, What is the brand or product that we want our community to purchase or con-sume? What is the identity we seek to portray? How are we creating an exchange between individuals and our community of faith?

It may be that we are sending unintentional messages that ask people to consume church instead of consuming Christ. Our brand is not a style of church; our brand is a lifestyle in the image of Jesus Christ. Our identity is *the person of Jesus Christ*. People do not want to consume an organization, institution, or set of traditions—but they will consume a lifestyle. By branding our churches instead of our lifestyle, we offer a product that is void of sustenance and vitality.

Church marketing focuses on what we *do*—what kind of music we play, how we preach, what programs we offer, what we wear, where we meet, when we meet, and what kind of coffee we drink.

Character Marketing

But there's another kind of marketing. *Character marketing* is the consistent process of displaying and performing the loving exchange between the church and individuals. The goal is to influence people through action to consume not an organization but the person of Christ (brand).

It will take a radically new approach to marketing if we are to overcome people's negative impressions of the church. Elaborate buildings, flashy marquees, trendy brochures, and convenient service times are not enough. Our marketing must speak louder than the static of reality TV, cell phones, iPods, and the demanding schedules of a widely distracted culture.

Character marketing focuses on who we are. Loving our community, caring for the weak, concerned about the poor, and accepting of others. It's about marketing the character of Christ, as well as your story of becoming more like Christ.

Even Jesus used character marketing. Withdrawing into the solitude of a nearby mountainside, Jesus gathered a crew of inexperienced disciples. Having captured their interest, he launched into the Beatitudes—teachings that provide an outline of the marks of a true disciple, in contrast to the attitudes of a person of the world. Jesus explained how these attitudes or character traits function as zest or flavor for all humanity: "You are the salt of the earth. But if the salt loses its saltiness, how can it be made salty again? It is no longer good for anything, except to be thrown out and trampled underfoot" (Matthew 5:13).

Salt serves to give flavor. Followers of Jesus are called to make the earth more savory. Not unlike Emeril Lagasse tossing his "essence" into the saucepan and shouting "Bam!" Jesus tosses his essence—in the form of his followers—into the melting pot of humanity and says, "Blessed!" (And I'm reasonably sure that most people would find the Food Network more palatable than whatever is on the platter of religious television at the moment.)

Jesus continued:

> You are the light of the world. A city on a hill cannot be hidden. Neither do people light a lamp and put it under a bowl. Instead they put it on its stand, and it gives light to everyone in the house. In the same way, let your light shine before others, that they may see your good deeds and glorify your Father in heaven.
>
> MATTHEW 5:14 – 16

Just as light has a distinctive impact on an environment, the follower of Jesus who stands out from the world will have a distinctive impact on it. But the motive for delectable and illuminating deeds is not to put a spotlight on our own virtue but to highlight its source.

It's sexy to be a social activist right now, but I caution the churches that are not helping people connect Jesus and compassion. Beware of recycled expressions of the social gospel that in many cases have lost sight of the gospel and allowed social reconstruction to become an end in itself. Jesus intended for the gospel to be social. It implies the social activism that has the goal of spiritual redemption. Social activism alone is just activism. But the gospel seasoned with loving activism is the truest form of compassion.

A perfect example is seen in the groundbreaking work of the Luis Palau Association in Portland. My good friend Kevin Palau shared with me their vision to utilize compassion and service as a backdrop for expressing the gospel in both word and deed. A few days ago, I sat with Kevin and a handful of other Christian leaders to brainstorm and help keep the momentum going that had been generated by the 2008 "Season of Service" that united Portland-area churches around five community concerns: homelessness, health and wellness, hunger and poverty, public schools, and the environment. It offered an entirely new focus on sustainable, repeatable, culturally relevant outreach opportunities.

The 2008 "Season of Service" drew 25,000 volunteers from churches across the city for projects that city leaders had selected. Hundreds of churches participated in food drives, public school cleanups, medical and dental clinic projects, and homeless service events. Collectively, churches participated in 278 projects over the Portland area. The support from community leaders was unprecedented, and this unique vision united churches all over the area. Even the area Wells Fargo banks set a goal of 10,000 employee volunteer hours. Kevin and the Palau team discovered, as *Christianity Today* writer Tim Stafford put it, that "American churches wanted a witness of service to go with verbal proclamation."[11]

Case Study

A few years ago, Grace Chapel made a significant shift in our marketing. We decided to market our character rather than our church. Instead of spending $10,000 on postcards and mailers, we decided to set a goal to raise $10,000 to address poverty and hunger in our community. Building on our relationships with public schools and community centers, we put a new spin on the classic rummage sale. The week before Easter, a local newspaper wrote a powerful story about the sale: "A local church finds that community needs reach beyond their own congregation. Kids who need glasses. Middle schoolers without coats. Residents who can't pay their electric bills. Somebody hears your cries and wants to do something about it."

The article—which happened to be better "marketing" than any postcard we could have sent—was the result of a deliberate strategy to depict the character of our church at a time (Easter) when people are most likely to think about church and whether or not it's something they want to include in their lives.

Our goal has been to link the church and the community by rallying around compassionate causes. We organize service projects twice a year, just prior to Christmas and Easter. We've discovered that during these highly commercialized seasons, people want to engage in something that makes a difference in the lives of others. Maybe this desire points to their particular way of trying to redeem the self-centered defacement of these sacred holidays. Either way, it's a great opportunity for our church. We began by asking, What is it that we want them to know about us at Grace Chapel—especially at a time when they might be thinking about church? Better yet, what is it that we want them to experience with us? It helped that plenty of media outlets crave stories of people who are demonstrating kindness in creative ways.

More Than Marketing

When I think of social entrepreneurism today, I think of four people: Bono, Oprah, Andy, and Serenity. You've probably heard of Bono and Oprah already, but the Coloumbes have their own radical infamy. I met Andy and Serenity Coloumbe a few years ago as we sat in the living room for the first night of our small group. Instantly there was a profound connection. We have experienced a lot together over the past few years.

One day, Andy and I were hanging out, and he said, "I think I want to do something for the homeless."

"What do you have in mind?" I asked with fascinated curiosity.

"I don't know, but I want to figure it out."

We agreed to talk about it in our small group. Coincidently, our group had just been discussing ways in which we could express the DNA of Christ in our lives. So one night, Andy shared his heart with our group members. This wasn't just some passing thought for Andy; it was a new conviction that would stimulate and stretch all of us in the group. A couple hours of provocative discussion unfolded into a plan. Andy and Serenity tossed the idea out there.

"Let's pack brown bags with food and pass them out."

I could sense everyone's interest being piqued.

"What about jackets?" another voice added to the mix.

"How about gloves?" asked another.

"Socks, scarves, beanies." More feedback.

It was settled. Andy and Serenity would coordinate a homeless venture, and the rest of the group agreed to be a part of it. For many, it proved to be their first experience of "Hanging with the Homies," as we would soon put it.

Later that week, the Coloumbes sent an email to the group detailing our game plan. We would meet at 3:00 p.m. to make sandwiches, pack bags, and load the vehicles. Cramming into our SUVs, we made the thirty-minute drive into downtown Portland. The conversation during the drive was invigorating and amusing. It was an adventure that was divinely orchestrated, not just for the Coloumbes, but for all of us.

As we drove around, deciding where to begin, memories from the seven years I had spent ministering in the area came back to me. (Our church plant and former duplex were only a few blocks away.) Amped-up on shared adrenalin, we were eager to leap out at the sight of the first person pushing a shopping cart. Armed with whole-wheat tuna sandwiches, apples, cookies, chips, and an arsenal of water bottles, we felt like an elite Special Forces unit.

As we walked the boulevard, we offered everything we had to anyone we encountered. The reality that any one of us could be walking in their shoes highlighted the thin, fragile line between destitution and lavishness. Our velvet-dress-and-chardonnay world had merged with one where cardboard is a commodity, newspapers are blankets, gutters are beds, and garbage is the carte du jour. It's a world where sex is a paycheck, starvation is waiting in line, abuse is entertainment, drugs are currency, sleep is art, sickness is dieting, shelters are vacation, and scavenging is shopping. That evening gave us a good look at the poverty around us—and a really good look at our prosperity.

That night gave birth to a burden that would continue to intensify within Andy and Serenity's hearts. Over the next several months, they made frequent excursions—through underpasses, alleys, gutters, and sidewalks. The grimace of these eroded faces uncovered the next episode of the journey that God was calling them to.

One evening, Andy and Serenity made an announcement to the group. "We want to travel the country visiting homeless shelters and loving the marginalized."

The room went quiet as everyone processed what this adventure would mean.

Andy interrupted the awkward silence. "We feel that God is calling us to sell our home, me to quit my job, and to buy an RV to live in as we travel across the nation serving at homeless shelters."

The hush was difficult to decipher. Some of us were excited and some were concerned. Everyone was sad at the prospect of losing our close friends. Over the next year, many of our conversations focused on the formation of their plans and their passion to take the love of Jesus Christ to the rejected and over-looked of society.

Many people in our church became inspired by the Coloumbes, including another young couple named Tim and Jen Fidanzo, who decided to join them on their trek from city to city.

Grace Chapel decided to support the Coloumbes and the Fidanzos officially as missionaries of our church. The moment we recognized them and commissioned them in front of the body, the entire crowd broke out in applause.

Compassion has a funny way of shaking things up, both in our personal faith and in our culture. The apathy of lukewarm Christianity starts to simmer with change when an authentic, radical love for Jesus expresses itself through acts of kindness.

The difference between leading a church and leading a movement is the ability to empower and fuel people to live out the love of Christ in ways that collide with the world of hurting people. We must stimulate those in our churches to be social entrepreneurs.

The Holy Spirit desires to ignite the body of Christ to be a torchbearer in a movement of committed concern. Imagine a community of faith willing to take the inherent risks of social enterprises and compassion ventures. The opportunities for us to change the world are within reach. The world would stand in awe at the marvelous sight of God's people revealing the type of divine love that once stained a cross.

Loving the Market

Getting your church to demonstrate compassion for those to whom you're marketing begins with knowing the heart of Jesus Christ. Consider the example of Jesus as he traveled through Capernaum with his disciples: "Jesus went through all the towns and villages, teaching in their synagogues, proclaiming the good news of the kingdom and healing every disease and sickness. When he saw the crowds, he had compassion on them" (Matthew 9:35–36).

Veiled within this account is a momentous revelation underlining remarkable aspects that disclose the motives for Jesus' compassion.

I'm not sure we fully understand the word *compassion* as used here to describe Jesus' heart for people. It would be a mistake to see it as simply synonymous with *empathy* or *sympathy*. It has a much more intense connotation than that. The Greek word for *compassion* is *splanchnizomai*, which literally means "to be moved as to one's bowels" or "to have the bowels yearn." This is different from the feeling you get when you eat a late-night jalapeño chili burger. It evokes the idea of a deep gut reaction and connotes allowing yourself to be moved by feelings of shared misery—so much so that you actually join with people in their agony.

In these two verses in Matthew 9, the gospel writer sketches a picture of Jesus making his way through the crowds of yoke-burdened people. I can hear the wailing of a woman who desperately cries for Jesus to heal her crippled son. I can feel the force of countless hands pressing toward Jesus in hope of deliverance. As it wafts its way toward me, I can smell the sordid stench of infected flesh. I can see the stare of despondency on the face of a little girl who sits alone, covered in the filth. And the Son of God, the Author of Life, the High Priest, the Good Shepherd, the Lamb of God—standing there in the epicenter of devastation and ruin.

Amid this scene, Jesus looks on a landscape of broken lives and allows himself to identify with their condition. His intense feeling of mutual anguish came from the simple act of observation. Jesus looked! He did not turn his back on the misery of those in anguish. Instead, he intently gazed at the crowd. Compassion is a gut response that wells up when we open our eyes to the misfortune of others.

Matthew explains what it was that Jesus saw that evoked his gut feeling of compassion: "Then [Jesus] said to his disciples, 'The harvest is plentiful but the workers are few. Ask the Lord of the harvest, therefore, to send out workers into his harvest field'" (9:37–38).

Those of us in ministry like to quote this passage, hoping it will summon a great response from the church. Jesus was right when he said "the workers are few." But why are there so few? Perhaps it's because we've replaced compassion with apathy. Jesus himself experienced compassion when he *saw* the crowds. Apathy sets in when we allow ourselves to remain unaware of conditions around us. Stimulating compassion is about replacing apathy with awareness.

Part of creating awareness is helping people be informed and well educated. This can be done through videos, websites, brochures, blogs, posters, and more. However, the best way to generate awareness is to give people opportunities to experience direct personal connection with someone in need. This goes beyond the offering plate and requires individual sacrifice.

A few years ago, I found myself being surrounded by a crowd of Rwandan street children in the capital city of Kigali. A friend of mine named Charles Buregeya is a pastor in Rwanda. Charles and his wife, Florence, had been part of our church plant while they were studying at Multnomah Bible College. For years, Charles had talked to me about visiting his church in Africa. Some other good friends, Tony and Serena, helped Charles form an organization called Africa New Life Ministries. They successfully built an orphanage that would be a place of refuge for the thousands of children orphaned by the 1994 genocide.

It was my first visit to Africa, and the first team our church had sent to Rwanda. A few days into the trip Matt, David, a few other team members, and I participated in a day camp for street children. In the midst of games, songs, balloons, and dancing, I noticed that David was really getting into it. He was a natural with the children, and they loved David the *muzungu* (Kinyarwandan for "crazy white person"). During one of the story times, as the children sat and listened, David and I stood over to the side, just taking it all in. I glanced at David and could tell something was on his mind. He had a look of sadness and grief on his face.

"How are you doing, man?" I asked.

As tears saturated his eyes, he exclaimed, "It hurts to see these kids in this condition. I have to do something more for them."

Clearly, David was aware of the sad condition that genocide had left these children in. His new awareness induced a strong emotional response. He was experiencing compassion. To this day, David will tell you that this moment in Rwanda transformed him forever. Visiting the orphanage that our church had helped build was breathtaking. For the first time, children had a place to sleep, a housemother to care for them, food to eat, access to health care, and the opportunity for an education. The contrast between the children on the street and those in the newly built orphanage justified every priceless cent supplied through child sponsorship.

Having seen firsthand what a few dollars a month can do for a child, we made a strategic inquiry. We wanted to know how many children were on a waiting list to be sponsored so that they could get off the street and into the orphanage. There were about a hundred. So we agreed to make it our goal to get all one hundred children sponsored immediately. A month after returning home, our staff came up with a plan to use a segment of our Sunday morning services to create awareness. By the end of that Sunday, all one hundred children had sponsors from our church. Since then, we have continued to make awareness a priority.

Not everyone can get on a plane and travel around the globe. But everyone can make an effort to step outside of their worlds and dispense hope and love (and we can help others to do the same). Whether it's sending teams to New Orleans, Mexico, Nicaragua, or Rwanda; building orphanages, hospitals, or water wells; redeeming those ensnared in sex trafficking; sponsoring or adopting a child; producing documentaries or building example shanties in our church lobby; collecting food for the poor or participating in disaster relief; sharing jackets and clothing with the homeless—we can create awareness, causing the worlds of those who are in need and those who can help meet needs to collide.

At Grace Chapel, we regularly hear about the impact one person has had on their entire small group after participating in a short-term mission trip. Even though only one or two people in the group actually get on a plane, the entire group takes part in the journey. Awareness is something that happens in a viral way through a network of relationships.

The ultimate objective for creating awareness is leading people to a greater understanding of the character of God. Becoming aware of global issues alone is news; becoming aware of the heart of God is revelation. The Bible inspires more compassion than all human aid groups combined.

Shared Market

A biblically inspired compassion can be experienced beyond church circles. Sometimes churches think they have a corner on the market for alleviating pain, suffering, disaster, and human tragedy. We need to wake up and realize that the world has every right to see a need and do something about it. It's one aspect of compatibility that all humanity shares.

One morning, as Grace Chapel's staff was brainstorming ways to address poverty and hunger in our community, we ran into a wall. As good as our intentions were, we had no idea where to start. It's not as though you can just approach a dilapidated house, knock on the door, and say, "Hey, you look like you might be impoverished. How can we help you?" The residents may have disheveled dwellings, but they still have dignity. Not only did we lack knowledge of where to start; we didn't even know what people needed.

After several frustrating hours of discussion, though, we had a breakthrough: *Call the schools.* (It's nice having a personal relationship with these hubs in the community.) So I got on the phone.

That next week, I sat in Katie's toy-filled office. She is the school counselor at one of our local public schools. "Katie, we need your help," I said.

"What did you have in mind?"

I tried to get comfortable in a chair meant to accommodate a third-grader. "We want to reach poor families in our community, but we don't know where to start. I thought maybe you would have an idea."

Katie's eyebrows lifted. "We have families coming to us every day needing food and clothing." She went on to explain that some of their buses even pick up children from the homeless community camped at a nearby rest stop. I even learned that one family was living in a horse stall. "But our school district doesn't see the local schools as a social service agency, so it won't provide funding to help us address these issues."

That got me. With pen and paper in hand, I asked, "What are the needs?"

I tried to keep up, writing down everything that she was listing off. Finally, I just got overwhelmed and realized there was more than what we could handle at one time.

Katie smiled. "I have a list of families, including names, clothing sizes, and specific needs."

Everything inside of me knew this was an extraordinary opportunity to become part of our strategy to reach the poor in our community. For the next hour, Katie and I discussed how we could connect our church's resources with her school's relationships. Katie's list of names and needs was long; it included jackets, shoes, gloves, pants, beanies, underwear, shampoo, toothbrushes, books, and socks. Once I had the list, I took it back to our team. Since it was early December, we decided to call our efforts a "Joy Drive."

Every school in our community loved the idea. Each one expressed the same dilemma that Katie faced. Hundreds of families from our community were looking to the schools to help meet their needs. Unfortunately, schools had their hands tied by budget constraints, even though many teachers were spending their own hard-earned money to help meet some of the needs. That Christmas, we collected lists from all of the schools and presented the vision to our church on a Sunday morning. Over the next few weeks, people loaded up boxes and bags, filling our lobby with every item on the list—and then some!

Once we had collected everything, our staff loaded the items into their vehicles and delivered them to the schools. Having our staff members walk the halls of every public school—arms overflowing with life's necessities—was truly a remarkable sight.

I am reminded of an amazing passage of Scripture:

> Is not this the kind of fasting I have chosen:
> to loose the chains of injustice
>   and untie the cords of the yoke,
> to set the oppressed free
>   and break every yoke?
> Is it not to share your food with the hungry
>   and to provide the poor wanderer with shelter—
> when you see the naked, to clothe them,
>   and not to turn away from your own flesh and blood?
> Then your light will break forth like the dawn,
>   and your healing will quickly appear.
>
> ISAIAH 58:6–8

True, there are many humanitarian organizations that aren't championing their causes for the sake of Jesus Christ.

The idea of partnering with them may make some Christians uncomfortable, because we assume that association with them will put us in bed with pagans and political activists. That's possible — in fact, it's likely. But just so you know that I'm not advocating "selling out," let me paint a picture for you.

Ever since the explosion of the parachurch movement, we've seen a change in how the church views compassion, resulting in a dichotomy of function. Single-focused ministries stepped out from under the control and shared resources of local churches. It is far more beneficial for nonprofit entities to branch off and focus their resources, budgets, staffing, and fund-raising underneath their own umbrellas. Local churches carried the function of carrying out worship services, while parachurch organizations took on the function of performing various specialized ministries.

Consider the Pregnancy Resource Center. My mother-in-law directs one of their facilities. What they do is amazing, but it takes an enormous amount of resources from several churches and individual Christians to pull it off. To consider bringing them under the wing of one local church would be foolish. This "separation" has served the parachurch movement well, but it has not served local churches well — at least not in terms of their reputations in their communities.

You and I understand that parachurch ministries and local churches are all part of the one holy, universal church. However, those in our community can't make sense of the intricate facets of local church/parachurch relationships. When the people in your community see your church, they see a building that facilitates the one- or two-hour gathering of people on a Sunday morning. What they don't see is your local church contributing financially and providing volunteers to all the amazing parachurch organizations across the world. And because the majority of these financial contributions and volunteers go directly to Christian organizations, the unchurched world has no idea you're even doing it.

I'm not advocating the abandonment of your partnerships with parachurch organizations. In fact, many churches have discovered that parachurch organizations are able to help them experience great PR as a result of their partnerships. I am simply suggesting that you broaden your associations to include organizations within your own community that may have no Christian roots.

The church *is* doing amazing things all over the world as it applies a soothing balm to relieve a variety of global hurts, mostly through parachurch organizations. A friend of mine is a successful CPA who runs in a circle of wealthy Christian businessmen. She made a thought-provoking comment to me recently: "Many of the wealthy businessmen I know are not giving money to their local church." When I asked why, she responded, "Because they don't think their churches are truly reaching out."

People in your church want to give to a cause, not for the developing of more programs or the paying of electric bills. The (typically) false perception that the church is not responding is shared by those both in the church and outside of it. The local church has become known to many as an uncaring, impotent club incapable of demonstrating itself to the world. It's our desire to do everything we can to make sure our community sees us making an all-out effort to address issues such as HIV/AIDS, hunger, poverty, disease, sex trafficking, clean water, the environment, and so on. It's time for the local church to reclaim its place as the source of inspiration for social justice and action.

Human rights is a leading issue on the table for discussion in our culture. Let's model the love of Jesus Christ in such a visible, tangible expression that it provokes others to discover the true motive behind our actions. Will you please take a seat at the table? There is an empty spot with your name on it.

6

the wounded beast

Gathering on Sundays

I received a call one afternoon from a friend teaching a class on church and culture at Multnomah Biblical Seminary. He was excited about the direction our church was heading.

"I'd like to have you talk with all of the graduate interns about what it means to do incarnational church work," he said. "Just tell them what you are trying to create at your church."

I was a bit hesitant at first. After all, I was still trying to figure it out myself. I didn't want to put my experiment under the scrutiny of graduate students.

The day arrived. I opened with the following remark: "I want each of you to pretend the church has no history and Jesus Christ has personally given you the assignment to go and make disciples." I followed up with this question: "With no church philosophy, models, or paradigms to rely on, how would you carry out this task?"

One student said, "I would share with my family first and then with all my friends. I would spend time with them over coffee or lunch discussing the new life I've experienced." Another student commented that he would spend time with a few individuals and devote his energy to their growth and life change. After several minutes of dialogue—and many more comments like these—I made an observation: None of the students had said a word about renting a school, hiring a band, getting a sound system, holding an event, or doing some mass marketing. Every answer came back with the idea of *personal relationship.*

Don't get me wrong. I am all for organized gatherings for worship and teaching. Such services are vital to the process. However, our method of introducing people to Jesus and building them up can't be reduced to a Sunday worship service. Why not discover the best process for engaging your culture, introducing people to Jesus, and building them up—and then ask, "Within this process, where does the Sunday service fit in and how?"

Eat Up!

If someone were to ask your church members to describe their church, how would they answer? Would they describe the functional elements of a worship service such as the music, teaching, liturgy, or the use of media? Or would they talk about the characteristics of a particular lifestyle such as serving, compassion, and community? A time has come when the church can no longer be defined by its weekend services. The ancient church—the first followers of Jesus—were defined not by a service but by a lifestyle.

When we embrace a narrow definition of the church—in other words, "something that happens on Sundays only"—we are left with a subconscious absence of spiritual fulfillment. It becomes easy to habitually drift in and out of worship services, wondering why we have mediocre and unfulfilling spiritual lives. Meanwhile, unbelievers respond by asking, "Is that all there is?"

To this narrow definition of the church we have added our consumerist "serve me" attitude. We look to weekend services for quick spiritual fixes—like an addict hoping to take another hit from the Bible bong. How often have you heard someone say, "We're looking for a church that meets our needs"? In response to this window-shopping mind-set, churches try to make themselves as appealing as possible. They no longer engage in efforts to reach culture; rather, it becomes all about beating the competition. We've created a religious marketplace characterized by convenient value meals and mediocre customer service. Our obsession to make church about *our* self-gratification and convenience has prostituted the gospel.

For far too long, the Sunday gathering has been a point of contention and controversy. Are we seeker sensitive or believer building? This question has perplexed church leaders for decades. Sadly, the unresolved debate has crippled the church. By focusing on the weekly gathering, we are handicapping our ability to function as the grown-up spiritual adults that God wants us to be. In the words of Paul to the Corinthians:

> Brothers and sisters, I could not address you as spiritual but as worldly—mere infants in Christ. I gave you milk, not solid food, for you were not yet ready for it. Indeed, you are still not ready. You are still worldly. For since there is jealousy and quarreling among you, are you not worldly?
>
> 1 CORINTHIANS 3:1–3

Such immaturity is captured in the juvenile expectation that worship services are "for me." Sadly, the focus has shifted from reaching the world to playing to my own wants. Instead of aligning our services around the surrounding culture, we align our services around our own preferences. Sometimes I'm tempted to hang a banner from the front of the church stage that reads, "Welcome, but it's *not* about you."

The spiritual offspring of a consumer Christian culture expects a buffet of enlightening delicacies. A self-absorbed perspective demands that churches offer a wide range of palatable options. We have become slaves to our own base appetites, and we have lost what makes us thriving followers of Jesus.

True growth happens as a result of responding to God's will for our lives. It happens when we exercise our faith. Consider the words of Jesus when approached by his disciples in Samaria shortly after he spoke with a woman at a well. He was tired and hungry from a wearisome journey when they decided to make a stop at a local well. The disciples left him to rest as they made a run to the nearby market. During their absence, Jesus engaged in an amazing interaction with a Samaritan woman. At the climax of this life-transferring exchange, the disciples returned with food and encouraged him to partake: "Rabbi, eat something." But Jesus replied, "I have food to eat that you know nothing about." The disciples looked at each other and wondered aloud, "Could someone have brought him food?" (John 4:31–33).

In that moment Jesus revealed what he had been feeding on: " 'My food,' said Jesus, 'is to do the will of him who sent me and to finish his work' " (John 4:34).

Notice that Jesus did not say that what fed him was listening to the compelling homily of a rabbi or the pleasurable discourse of a religious guru. Jesus wasn't interested in munching on pseudofood with artificial flavoring. He was ingesting the spiritual edibleness of God's mission for his life. Jesus said that when his life aligned with God's missional call, his soul was fed. The residue of modernism has led us to believe that spiritual growth occurs in the mind only.

When Jesus asked Peter to feed his sheep (see John 21), he implied that Peter (and others) would share the same source from which Jesus found his nourishment. What Jesus had in mind for feeding or tending was the embraced missional calling of Jesus, not just the dispensing of biblical information. Shepherds don't just tell their sheep where to find food; nor do they feed them out of their hands. Shepherds lead sheep to a pasture to graze. For us, this means going beyond weekend services. Making the shift between leading a church and leading a movement demands a willingness to change the way we define *being fed*. Weekend services then become part of the feeding process but aren't equated with it. Our weekend gatherings can then be freed to become a significant part of the transitioning into a missional journey.

You're in My Space

Every August, millions of college students flood campuses to face an overwhelming wave of classes, student loans, and ridiculously pricey textbooks. Perhaps the biggest pressure awaits in the dorm room—the new roommate. We hope we get along. We want someone who is fun but not rowdy, clean but not obsessive-compulsive; we're looking for someone who likes our style of music—and most of all for someone who won't make a move on my main squeeze.

Living in a shared space can be tense. It only works when everyone respects, enjoys, and values the presence of the other people. It certainly requires accepting that it's not always going to be about me.

The shared space at church—most notably the worship service—is populated by people whose spiritual journeys run across the whole spectrum. Sometimes I sit back and reflect on the characters who attend our weekly gatherings. They are so diverse and can even be opposite personalities. It's sometimes like a scene from *The Odd Couple*—and yet it's wonderful.

Church leaders should make no distinction between insiders or outsiders. It's not about seekers or believers; it's about people. Besides, aren't we all seekers? Our message is the same to everyone: know Jesus, love Jesus, and follow Jesus. Preaching Jesus is relevant to any spiritual seeker, whether pre- or postconversion.

If church is defined as a process and not an event, then weekend gatherings can be utilized as another piece of the strategic process of life change. The church is not meant to be a place of dormancy but of constant motion. Weekend gatherings can be maximized as revolving doors, linking the ideas of receiving from the community and sending into it.

Our weekend gatherings at Grace Chapel function within our "park" environment. The purpose of this environment is to connect the body of Christ to those from the culture in which we live. It's the continuation of the relational thread. It's moving along the process from "engaging with them in culture" to "including them in community." Our goal is to help those in the surrounding culture feel welcome and accepted as a part of our broader faith community. Once this happens, we strive to make meaningful introductions—connecting them with Jesus and introducing them to others who are journeying along the same spiritual highway.

Our larger get-togethers are an invitation to "come and see," connected to an invitation to "come and follow." As Jesus ministered in a particular place, crowds would come and see what he was about. It became an environment for them to discover the spiritual truths that Jesus championed. Of course, during these encounters, Jesus offered the opportunity to move beyond being a spectator to becoming a follower. Likewise, weekend gatherings are about helping people cross from unbelief into belief. We can eliminate many barriers when we align our expectations around this principle that Paul speaks of in 1 Corinthians:

> So if the whole church comes together and everyone speaks in tongues, and inquirers or unbelievers come in, will they not say that you are out of your mind? But if an unbeliever or an inquirer comes in while everyone is prophesying, they are convicted of sin and are brought under judgment by all, as the secrets of their hearts are laid bare. So they will fall down and worship God, exclaiming, "God is really among you!"
>
> 1 CORINTHIANS 14:23–25

Notice the transitional nature of their gatherings. By creating a comfortable environment without compromising the integrity of God's word, the church includes the unbeliever in its gathering, inviting him or her to move from unbelief to belief. It's obvious that Paul has embraced the idea of unbelievers joining with Christians for their "worship services." But he goes even further, implying that their gatherings should function with unbelievers in mind. I love the fact that Paul essentially told the Corinthian church to chill out when it came to behaving in a way that would make outsiders think they were nuts! Instead of conducting a religious freak show, the believers are encouraged by Paul to let God's word penetrate the depths of people's souls, underscoring their need for a Savior.

First Impressions

When I was in college, my brother-in-law talked me into selling Kirby vacuum cleaners. He was convinced we would make a ton of cash, so I agreed. I will never forget my first sales meeting.

Larry, the district manager, led me into the grungy, unkempt room on the second floor of a dingy office building. A collection of shady characters opened the sales meeting by singing a song that went like this, "Hail, hail, the gang's all here, the guys who sell the Kirby!" I think it was sung to the tune of an old hymn. I couldn't stop laughing as tone-deaf bellowing filled the room. After the worship set was done, Larry pulled out some lime-green fuzzy dice, which were part of a tacky incentive program. If you had made a sale the day before, you were given the opportunity to roll double-or-nothing against the boss for twenty bucks.

Next came the sales training lecture. A highly motivated sales rep preached the gospel of the Kirby vacuum and its redemptive mission to take away the tarnished stains of carpet filth. There was even a greeting time after the meeting for people to get to know each other. One guy asked me to join him at a nudie bar.

I went home that day convinced they were all loony. This was my first impression of the Kirby gathering. It was also my last impression.

When Paul cautioned the Corinthians to not do anything that made them appear out of their minds, he was talking about first impressions. Our weekend gatherings have to consider what kind of impression they leave. First impressions form in just a glance—maybe three seconds. In the first few moments of every new encounter, others are evaluating you. They are forming opinions based on your appearance, mannerisms, demeanor, body language, and clothing style. To make such appraisals is to be human.

It can be difficult to control the first impressions that unbelievers have of believers, but there are things we can do to help shape them. Unfortunately, we must also consider the likelihood that many unbelievers have already had a negative first impression of a church gathering. Sometimes our first impressions must be arranged to re-impress them and deconstruct their negative perceptions of the church.

Since we see our weekend church gatherings as an opportunity for first impressions, we invest countless efforts and resources into creating an environment that is both *inviting* and *inspirational*. These two words describe what Grace Chapel's Sunday morning "park" environment is all about. Within these words are a number of lessons on making first impressions that last. Let's look at just a few.

Include People

The gatherings that occur within our "park" environment are designed to be places of universal acceptance—entry points into the larger community of faith. These are places where prostitutes, zealots, tax collectors, thieves, religious, rich, and destitute alike can assemble to absorb God's message of grace and truth.

To help those in our churches to become inviters, we must create a safe environment that gives them complete confidence that their guests will be welcomed and accepted. There's a significant distinction between churches that say, "What do you believe? OK, now you belong," and those that say, "You belong. Now what do you believe?" Because church gatherings are typically the first introduction to the Christian community, it's vital to create an environment that is conducive to inclusion.

Be Authentic

Authenticity is about an expression of genuine sincerity that empowers others to trust. Because trust is something that has to be earned, it's vital to create an atmosphere of sincerity. Fake, contrived, disingenuous, phony, inauthentic—these may be the impressions many people (both unbelievers and believers) have of the church.

Several years ago, a pastor-friend of mine walked through one of the most depressing seasons of his life. No longer could he get in front of his church on Sunday and pretend to be something he wasn't. He was tired and worn-out from years of ministry. His spiritual life had been running on fumes.

One particular Sunday, as his alarm clock announced the dawning of a new day, he came face-to-face with the reality that he had nothing more to give. Instead of putting on another false veneer and preaching a contrived message, he shared the truth with his congregation. Standing in front of his church, he bared his soul, exposing the truth buried deep within his heart. The church leadership extended the opportunity for a much-needed sabbatical—during which time the church experienced continued numerical and spiritual growth.

When I asked this pastor why this church kept growing during his absence, he said that something historic had been discovered in his church, namely, authenticity. People came because the word on the street was this was an authentic church that gave people room to be honest with themselves, each other, and God. Inclusion comes more naturally when people move past their facades and experience the freedom that sincerity brings.

Validate Others

Validation is one of the most important emotional skills. If we want to create an environment that fosters inclusion and encourages better relationships, validation can be extremely useful. Validation is the ability to communicate one powerful sentiment: "I can't pretend to understand everything you're feeling, *but I do care.*" It means demonstrating that we will still accept others after they've shared their feelings — even when they're raw and anguished.

We let others know we respect their view of things. We make them feel heard, acknowledged, understood, and accepted. Sometimes this takes the form of just plain good listening. Sometimes it's a nod or some other sign of understanding; other times it can take the form of a hug or a gentle touch. Sometimes validation means being patient when the other person just isn't ready to talk. Validation does not require condoning another's behavior or attitude. But when pastors and their congregations practice the art of listening, others will experience a profound sense of validation that can propel their inclusion into the community.

Create the Right Atmosphere

Atmosphere sets the mood of a gathering. People will feel either a sense of inclusion or an impression of exclusivity. The big question is, "Do people feel welcomed in this atmosphere?" Have you ever been in an environment that made you feel so uncomfortable that you swore you would never return? Our churches have to create the opposite feeling.

The ability to create an environment of belonging is captured in the ancient understanding of hospitality. Paul in Romans 12:13 urges followers of Jesus to "practice hospitality," but what does this mean? The Greek word *philoxenia*, translated as "hospitality," means "love to strangers." It's more than just a handshake or the friendly delivery of a church bulletin. In order to understand the true idea of hospitality, we must return to a more generous era of social interaction.

In the days of the early church, hospitality was of the utmost importance. Strangers passing outside of a home could be invited inside. The host would wash the strangers' feet and offer food and wine; only after being made to feel comfortable would the guests be asked their names. Hospitality is about making strangers and hosts equal, making the former feel protected and taken care of and guiding them safely to their next destination.

Inclusion happens when we go out of our way to make strangers feel accepted and loved.

Touch Others

Little do we realize that people who attend our weekly gatherings are hungry for personal affection. Recently, a woman who had been visiting our church for a while approached me after worship. She asked if I had a few moments to talk with her about some challenges she was experiencing in her relationship with God. She mentioned how difficult it was for her to read her King James Bible—the only one she owned. In my mind, there was an easy solution. I walked with her to our guest information kiosk and handed her a modern version of the Bible. Honestly, it wasn't that big of a deal. I figured anyone else would have done the same.

A week later, one of her friends approached me to let me know how touched she was that I had taken the time to invest in her needs. Apparently she was blown away by the gesture of finding her a new Bible and the hug that I gave her. I'm not sure what is more distressing—that it's rare to get that type of personal touch or that I passed it off as not a big deal.

Something about human affection speaks to our fragile emotional need for inclusion. The Bible tells us to "greet one another with a holy kiss" (Romans 16:16) and reminds us through the example of Jesus of the importance of physical touch (see, for example, Matthew 8:3, 15; Mark 10:16). American culture today

suffers from an attachment disorder. The symptoms of this disorder can be treated by creating a warm environment that fosters
seeking proximity through appropriate physical touch. Handshakes and hugs convey love, reverence, and esteem.

Laugh

I am sure you have heard it said that "laughter is the best medicine." The sound of thundering laughter is more contagious
than any sneeze or cough. Humor has a way of causing joy and
happiness to spread. Even in the most difficult times, a laugh or
a chuckle can go a long way in helping us feel better. Every area
of our lives—our work, our marriage, and our family—needs
humor and laughter.

Belonging to a community means making it through hard-
ship together and laughing together. Humor binds us together
in a way that lightens our burdens and keeps things in perspective. We all experience seasons of trouble and difficulty;
such times demand so much energy, focus, and effort from us.
Amusement is a coping mechanism that enables us to press on
though these difficult times.

Joy is a frequently mentioned aspect of the Christian life.
Our joy becomes more complete as we include each other in the
fellowship of faith. When we laugh with one another, it binds
us together in a profound way. Laughter has a way of tearing
down walls; the more these walls come down, the easier it is for
people to include each other.

Create a Safe Place

Going to church can be a big risk, especially if someone is
unfamiliar with all the ins and outs of church culture. Creating
a climate where people feel safe to experiment and explore

without judgment or criticism is vital. This can only happen by releasing individuals to respond without feeling obligated to do so. We create safe gatherings when others feel welcome to engage at their own pace.

As I was growing up, I was taught to focus on saying a prayer, raising a hand, or going forward during the altar call. It was all about instant salvation. The spotlight was on the moment of decision—on conversion.

In his book *The Church on the Other Side*, Brian McLaren helps us see another way of thinking of conversion, as he reminds us of the importance of creating a safe place in our churches.

> The conversion event will be seen in the new church as a snapshot of a flowing river, a rain shower in a larger weather system, an important episode in an all-important process.
>
> As a result, we won't rush people toward a decision. We will see rushed decisions as potential abortions—harmful, dangerous, even criminal.[12]

A safe environment will keep us from rushing people into something they are not ready for. Many unbelievers hesitate to attend church because they're afraid—usually for good reason—that they will be expected to do something they are not ready to do.

Think about the feeling you get as you pull up to a car dealership and you know that salesmen will be hovering in packs like hungry vultures, hoping to feast on naïveté and good credit. I hate going car shopping for this very reason. I want the freedom to just look around without feeling pressured. In the same way, guests at your church will allow themselves to be included when they feel confident that they're not going to be attacked by insistent sales pitches.

Inspire Others

What's the difference between telling people what to believe and moving them to believe? Everything. Inspiration is the new apologetic. Note the words of Peter to the scattered believers in Asia: "Always be prepared to give an answer to everyone who asks you to give the reason for the hope that you have. But do this with gentleness and respect" (1 Peter 3:15).

The ability to give an answer or reasonable explanation for the hope we have is labeled *apologetics*. Today, our apologetic is shifting from a didactic position to an experiential one, from one that is information driven to one that is inspiration driven.

Inspiration is not just about the sermon; it's about the whole of worship. It's more than just stimulating the mind; it's about stimulating the whole person. Creating an environment that inspires people to follow Jesus is like choreographing a symphony of heartbeats deep within our souls.

Inspiration shows no bias between those who believe and those who skeptically await a reason to take a step of faith. Inspiration is about moving each person one step forward from wherever they are in their spiritual journey. To create an ethos of inspiration, you must establish resonance and move people by painting a compelling image of what *could* be. Every component of your gatherings must embody what you are calling others to.

Weekly church gatherings can be powerful. Something amazing happens when the larger community of faith draws together in a common space. This setting offers the opportunity to create an experience that provokes someone to leave behind a life of peripheral spirituality and embark on an adventure of Christ-centeredness instead.

Communicate

In an image-saturated world, communication must evolve beyond the spoken word only. A world of ubiquitous visual stimulation currently inundates our consciousness.

Also, we can no longer assume that every person sitting in a church pew subscribes to a Christian worldview. Addressing the mind was the rhetoric of the modern communicator, whereas petitioning the heart is the vernacular of the postmodern message.

People are looking to experience a higher power or source of enlightenment. Because of this desire for authority, the Bible must become central to the message. During the seeker-sensitive craze of the past few decades, teaching and preaching minimized the use of Scripture and focused more on life principles, sprinkled with occasional references to a Bible verse. In a spiritually dehydrated culture like ours, it's important to remember that the Bible is not a springboard for a common-sense annotation. The Word of God functions as a penetrating sword that cuts to the very core of our being. It reveals the mysteries of God and stimulates us to respond in faith.

Communicating to a postmodern culture necessitates placing Jesus, not our felt needs, at the center of our message. Instead of communicating Jesus as a response to a crisis, we must communicate Jesus beyond our crises. The message of the redemptive story is told through the use of redemptive analogies — and the communicator is a raconteur of this romantic message.

Have Passion

The meaning of the word *passion* varies from person to person. Passion can be defined as "an entire range of strong emotions," especially love, lust, heat, rage, mania, and sexual desire. Even the agony of Jesus at the crucifixion is described as the *passion* of Christ. Ultimately, passion is something that comes from within. When we have a passion for something, we want to attain that particular something at any cost.

People look to soak up a spirituality. Authentic passion is not something that can be simulated; it must come from a genuine desire for someone or something. Even though true passion cannot be contrived, it can be caught. Because passion is caught and not taught, we must demonstrate what it looks like to pursue Jesus Christ with passion. Passionate people invigorate others. They spread an enthusiasm to live—to truly live.

Ultimately, it is God's Spirit who stirs a passionate response in the hearts of people, but he uses the stories and lives of extraordinary people to inspire. When writing to the Corinthians, Paul remarked on this transference of passion: "Follow my example, as I follow the example of Christ" (1 Corinthians 11:1).

Live in Expectation

Mysteries are something secret, unexplainable, obscure, or puzzling. Creating an environment that inspires people to show up with an attitude of anticipation requires us to reinstate the mystery of spontaneity. I think of the story of Zechariah, who was given the responsibility of burning incense.

> Once when Zechariah's division was on duty and he was serving as priest before God, he was chosen by lot, according to the custom of the priesthood, to go into the temple of the Lord and burn incense. And when the time for the

burning of incense came, all the assembled worshipers were praying outside.

Then an angel of the Lord appeared to him, standing at the right side of the altar of incense. When Zechariah saw him, he was startled and was gripped with fear.

LUKE 1:8–12

Apparently, Zechariah wasn't expecting a spontaneous visitation by an angel. The angel's presence alarmed him, causing him to react in fear. Zechariah had experienced the unexpected. Imagine what would happen if the church anticipated the visitation of God as his people gathered in his name. Imagine the buzz of God's people reverberating with anticipation for the revelation of God's presence. God often speaks through a word of revelation to bless, encourage, or direct; he often prompts his people to pray, testify, or ask for prayer.

Worship

When we speak of worship in the context of "church services," we are considering just one aspect of worship. In his letter to the Romans, Paul connected the purpose of worship with how we live our lives: "Therefore, I urge you, brothers and sisters, in view of God's mercy, to offer your bodies as a living sacrifice, holy and pleasing to God—this is true worship" (Romans 12:1).

It's also important to note that worship was meant to be expressed within the context of community. Community is where believers have the opportunity to go beyond our isolated worlds in the hope of encountering God together. We want to feel God and be touched by him.

Creating an inspirational environment is about facilitating a connection between the Creator and his creation. Nothing else on the planet is as inspiring and moving as God's people shouting, raising hands and voices, or bowing silently in awe-filled reverence to honor the one and only living God. Our declaration of God's majesty will echo through eternity. Passion should characterize the nature of our worship. Anything less would be insolent.

Look at every culture on the planet, and you will discover that human beings were born to worship. Whether people admit it or not, they are worshiping something or someone—most likely themselves. By participating in authentic worship, believers remove themselves (or whatever other master they've put in the position of honor) from the throne and place the Holy One in that space instead.

Often, music and visual images aid in experiencing the truth of God during corporate worship. Worship services have become increasingly visual as churches use art to illustrate truth in powerful ways. Within the emerging postmodern culture, people want more than just entertaining bands. They want to move beyond entertainment to authentic engagement. They don't want a phony, slick wannabe-rock-star worship leader. They desire to be led to an encounter with God by those who genuinely know what it's like to experience his presence. As we utilize both music and visuals, we inspire people to come into his courts with praise.

From Park to Coffee Shop

Within the "park" environment, Sunday morning gatherings are designed to be a place of transition. Since it's our goal to move people from the cultural community and into Christian community or missional small groups, we need a "next step" environment for them to transition into. For many people, moving beyond Sundays into a "living room" environment is too big of a step. Anticipating that, we created a temporary environment known as the "coffee shop," where people are given the chance to engage beyond Sunday mornings. This last year we started using the phrase "beyond Sundays" to help people understand that sitting in a pew is just the beginning of their community experience. Life in community is not about being passive or docile; it points to the risk of moving into more vulnerable and transparent friendships. Let's face it, unless you're proficient at eHarmony, the thought of moving from the copious crowd into intimate relationships is daunting—unless, of course, you've created an environment to help people discover their communal heritage. We call that environment the "coffee shop."

Part 3

the coffee shop

7

a rabbi, a muzungu, and the twilight zone

Passing into the Communal Dimension

It's Central Perk, the trendy establishment where the characters of *Friends* gather to download the humdrum of everyday life. It's Vesuvio Café just off Jack Kerouac Alley, where Mike Myers recites his beat poetry in *So I Married an Axe Murderer*. It's Café le Procope, the center of brilliant convergence and the birthplace of the *Encyclopédie*, the first modern encyclopedia—popularized by Voltaire, Benjamin Franklin, John Paul Jones, and Thomas Jefferson.

It's the coffee shop.

Today the idea of a coffee shop usually suggests a cozy, chic watering hole that offers gourmet espresso drinks and velvet sofas to lounge in while you sip. Whether or not you're sweet on the seductive dark brew, you'll most likely admit that coffee shops have an ethos of an affinity surrounding them. The expansive environment welcomes many different patrons—the young, the aged, the upscale, the simple, the artsy, and the professional. From a cultural perspective, coffeehouses function as centers for social interface, providing customers a place to meet, talk, read, express, connect, or relax.

Since the fifteenth century and originating from the Middle East, the coffee shop has served as a social gathering place for centuries. In recent years, its relational influence has broadened in Europe and the United States. The coffee shop culture is about interacting with people. Connection can be found in a cup.

I have to admit that I'm not a big coffee drinker. Never have been. So it's kind of ironic that I contribute so much revenue to coffee shops. As a pastor, I frequent coffee shops and cafés on such a habitual basis that I could keep Captain Ahab's first mate popular for a very long time. (This probably makes no sense unless you know the origins of a little Northwest-based coffee shop.)

There is no discrimination at the coffee shop. I can see a middle-aged man with multiple body piercings, sporting a faded leather jacket and a long, silvery ponytail. Two women sit a few tables away, laughing and erupting with hand gestures. Across the room, seated under a stylish lamp, two men exchange conversation characterized by mutual concern. It's difficult to make out what they are talking about, but the display of several empty cups suggests a weighty subject matter. A cluster of business associates are amusing themselves, sharing the paradoxes of parenting. A line forms and meanders around the obvious displays of coffee paraphernalia, and while jazz music plays in the background, baristas brew their admission ticket to social interface.

Smaller and more interactive than Grace Chapel's "park" environment, our "coffee shop" environment creates opportunities to form meaningful friendships. The coffee shop serves as a perfect metaphor for illustrating the concept of relational process.

Speed Dating

Probably the most popular speed-dating company out there is 8minuteDating.com. Their mission is "to provide the best way for people to establish relationships that add meaning to their lives." They promise a "fast, fun, safe, and comfortable" way for people to meet one another. Tired of the bar scene, pickup lines, blind dates, and guessing games, Tom Jaffee recognized that the singles population needed a better way to meet new and interesting people—and so he formed 8minuteDating.com.

Rabbi Yaacov Deyo invented the concept of speed dating as a way to help Jewish singles hook up. Coincidently in 1998 the first ever speed-dating event took place at a coffee shop called Pete's Café in Beverly Hills. What I like about speed dating is that it seeks to remove all of the awkwardness of approaching a total stranger and opening with a cheesy pickup line, such as, "Did you have Lucky Charms for breakfast? Because you look magically delicious!"

The advantage of speed dating is that it increases the chance of making connections, based on the fact that you're conversing with a number of people in one night. A conventional date requires spending an entire evening with one person, whereas speed dating facilitates multiple conversations. It's meant to be a transitory experience—providing a safe environment in which people can feel things out before they commit. If a connection is made, the couple meets again and takes the relationship to the next level.

Sometimes I feel like I'm in the speed-dating business. As new people attend a local church, the pressure is on to help them connect as quickly as possible. The clock is running. The longer it takes for new people to connect, the more skeptical they become about belonging. Church services can

be relationally awkward—like sitting at a table in a bar populated by fortysomething divorcées and gray-haired men while
the entire Cat Stevens collection pours out of the speakers. At
church we say things like, "Turn and greet the person next to
you," creating an unrealistic expectation that people will connect within those few seconds. Turning and greeting may help
create a friendly atmosphere, but it's not the ultimate way to
help people discover deep relational connectedness.

Plugging In

A few years ago, our church did a sermon series titled "The Living Room: Where Life Happens," with the purpose of motivat-
ing people to move beyond the Sunday services and enter into
community with each other. The response was overwhelming.
Immediately we had nearly 80 percent of our church plugged
into "Life Groups." As our church has grown since then, we
have continued to see people engage in community at approxi-
mately the same rate—and our groups have doubled in number
since the first day we unleashed them.

As exciting as this is, we are continually seeking to understand why some people still won't make an effort to belong.
We have a vision to see people passionately following Jesus
through the expression of community. Nothing frustrates me
more than watching those who confess faith in Jesus sit on the
sidelines and miss the opportunity to experience something
miraculous.

There have been hundreds of times when I wanted to get
up on stage and shout to everyone about going "all in." In those
moments, I imagine myself courageously, perhaps obnoxiously,
challenging people to get off their spiritually obese butts and
start being the church that God intended. (I know I would

never say it, but it helps just sharing it with you.) There is something inside of me that is tired of playing the church game. Eighty percent isn't good enough! I want to see entire churches so ignited for God that they align their entire existence around a reckless communal response to him.

The tension between seeing what could be and the reality of what is can be enough to make me want to throw in the towel. But as challenging as it may be, the experience of building authentic community is worth every effort. Watching a person who doesn't "get it" transition to "embracing it" is deeply satisfying.

Unplugging

Shepherding others to follow Jesus means understanding why some people are not engaging. As shepherds, it's our responsibility to discover why people get lost in the transition to full community. By doing this we can be more intentional at helping them overcome their barriers to belonging. Through endless discussions, feedback from other leaders, and personal observations, I am growing to understand some of the perspectives that dam people up and keep them from experiencing meaningful relationships.

Complacency

Complacency is the lullaby to the church. Complacency often stems from misguided contentment or unwarranted arrogance—feeling that we've arrived or wanting to be in the lead. Complacency is birthed out of comfort—and we live in a country that idolizes the pursuit of personal comfort. The American dream embraces the idea that you can acquire everything you need to enjoy a cushy lifestyle. Maintaining this way of life is all about deceiving ourselves into thinking that we don't need to rely on anyone else.

Spiritual complacency results when we take a casual approach to our relationship with God. We want just enough of what he offers to keep our lives comfortable. Heaven forbid that we sacrifice our time, resources, energy, or precious possessions for the sake of engaging more deeply with Christ or his body.

It's easy to rationalize such complacency when we compartmentalize our spirituality. We give God only a sliver of our lives and withhold the rest, while patting ourselves on the back and saying, "I've done enough," or "I'm good enough," or "I've given enough." Consider the warning Jesus gave to the Laodicean church:

> These are the words of the Amen, the faithful and true witness, the ruler of God's creation. I know your deeds, that you are neither cold nor hot. I wish you were either one or the other! So, because you are lukewarm—neither hot nor cold—I am about to spit you out of my mouth. You say, "I am rich; I have acquired wealth and do not need a thing." But you do not realize that you are wretched, pitiful, poor, blind and naked.
>
> REVELATION 3:14 – 17

In essence, the follower of Jesus who settles for complacency is like a divine loogey spit from the mouth of God. Actually, a more accurate translation of the image in Revelation would be "the act of vomiting." In other words, the lukewarm attitude of the church makes Jesus want to puke!

Let me be the first person to admit that I struggle with this kind of complacency. I strive for personal comfort. I commit the sin of mediocrity. In his New Testament letter, James says, "So then, if you know the good you ought to do and don't do it, you sin" (James 4:17). That's me. I know the good I ought to do, but all too often I don't do it. Even the apostle Paul confessed to this battle of a willing spirit versus weak flesh (see Romans 7). There is hope, though, as we press in to the one who can move us from complacency to accomplishment.

Individuality

America is a nation of individuals committed to individualism. It is the core concept enshrined in our national documents—that each of us would be free to pursue our own happiness and aspirations.

Not surprisingly, while living under the banner of rugged individualism, we have become the loneliest nation in the world.

The other day, I was having a discussion with someone in our church. As the conversation shifted from ordinary life events to deeper things, hc made a revealing statement: "I'm all for people joining groups, but it's not for me. I don't like people and what they require of me."

This comment seems to nail the way in which many people see it—as they hold to the doctrine that individuals ought to do what is in their own self-interest.

It's not that I'm against all aspects of individuality. Community and individualism are not mutually exclusive. We can be connected in a community without losing our identity. We individuals can be responsible to others. We can give and receive care, encouragement, and commitment. We can share a common purpose and a common sacrifice—all while remaining individuals. But in community we have the support of other believers, the mutual stimulation that others provide as we experience life together.

Notice what the apostle Paul penned to his close friends in Philippi as he encouraged them to reject the trademarks of an individualistic society:

If you have any encouragement from being united with Christ, if any comfort from his love, if any common sharing in the Spirit, if any tenderness and compassion, then make my joy complete by being like-minded, having the same love, being one in spirit and of one mind. Do nothing out of selfish ambition or vain conceit. Rather, in humility value others above yourselves, not looking to your own interests but each of you to the interests of the others.

In your relationships with one another, have the same attitude of mind Christ Jesus had:

Who, being in very nature God,
    did not consider equality with God something to be
    used to his own advantage;
rather, he made himself nothing
    by taking the very nature of a servant,
    being made in human likeness.
And being found in appearance as a human being,
    he humbled himself
    by becoming obedient to death—
        even death on a cross!

PHILIPPIANS 2:1–8

Community is not just about connecting individual pew fillers; it's about placing people into an environment where they have the opportunity to apply the attitude of Jesus Christ.

Busyness

Perhaps more than anything else, what keeps people from engaging in community is our ability to fill our schedules with more activities than time could possibly allow. Busyness is the

social constipation that prevents people from experiencing connectedness. The church needs an ex-lax moment!

When I landed at the Kigali airport in Rwanda a few years
ago, I was waiting at the customs window, fatigued and covered in sweat, when I noticed two official-looking men wearing
cobalt uniforms staring at me and mumbling the word *muzungu*.
My friend Tony whispered that the word meant "white person"
in Swahili. (I was just relieved to learn it didn't mean "cavity
search.")

Continuing through customs and pausing in the lobby long
enough to lather myself in 90 percent concentrated mosquito
repellant (it was the height of malaria season, and I had strict
orders from my health care provider), I heard it again: *Muzungu!*
I glanced over to see a well-dressed Rwandan woman snickering
at me. "*Muzungu*," she said, "no mosquito in Kigali."

Wearing my imaginary sash with the word *Idiot* on it,
I marched through the sliding glass doors to hear that word
again: *Muzungu*. It was a posse of men speaking to each other as
they swung machetes rhythmically through the weeds. Then as
we drove down the crowded terra-cotta streets, small children
swarmed around our minivan chanting, "*Muzungu, Muzungu!*"

Being a minority for perhaps the first time in my life, I must
have heard that word *muzungu* a thousand times during the
remainder of my visit to Rwanda. It wasn't until I arrived home
that I was told the full meaning of the word: "*crazy* white person." When Rwandans observe Americans, they think of chick-
ens running around with their heads cut off. Compared to their
culture, we are so busy that we actually appear to be insane.

Busyness characterizes the lives of most Americans. Family
obligations, career responsibilities, social activities, PTA meetings, soccer practices, Cub Scout projects, vacations, recitals,
deadlines, business trips. The push for more, more, and more

leaves us with less, less, and less. Most of our busyness results from a series of seemingly inconsequential demands that collectively become overwhelming. The real issue with busyness is not one of time management; it has to do with what we allow to dominate our attention — and what room is left for engaging in biblical community. We strive to create "the good life" while foolishly allowing ourselves to be distracted from the very thing that can provide it. Henry David Thoreau once wrote, "It is not enough to be busy; so are the ants. The question is: What are we busy about?"

While surfing the blogosphere, I discovered a website titled "Sacred Salvage." The blogger, JoshB, is committed to a vision of redeeming what the world decides to discard. The idea is to find something of value within the unseen, scarred, and the tarnished — to help break the silence and take a stand in declaring that lives are not disposable. This site inspired me to see community as a redeeming agent in the act of salvaging the sacred bond that transpires within the shared lives of the followers of Jesus.

What I found so fascinating about the Rwandan culture was their sense of community and lack of distraction. Relationship was a priority. Even men walked hand in hand down the street. The value they place on community, which no doubt runs deep and wide, was enhanced as an outcome of the suffering they endured during the national genocide.

Our love for the fast-paced treadmill, our addiction to doing more and more, has gone too far; our obsession has become a form of idolatry. Our perverse value reveals itself in those moments when we say, almost with pride, "I am really busy."

These words from the New Testament letter to the Hebrews can serve as a warning of the consequences of our busyness: "Let us consider how we may spur one another on toward love and good deeds, not giving up meeting together, as some are in the habit of doing, but encouraging one another — and all the more as you see the Day approaching" (Hebrews 10:24–25).

We can debate about whether or not the "meeting together" meant a worship service or the small gatherings that took place in people's homes in the days of the early church. The point is that when believers fail to get into the habit of connecting, we miss the opportunity to spur one another on and to encourage each other.

Note that the writer of Hebrews believed that connection was "all the more as you see the Day approaching." Christ's return is certainly more imminent today than it was when Hebrews was written, yet the American church has become more isolated, disconnected, and fragmented. Christ is going to return to a body that is overdosing on Red Bull instead of indulging in the tang of community.

It's easy to believe that the key to being good parents is being caught up in the busyness of our children's extracurricular activities. But as author and theologian Jim Wallis observes:

> What would a more biblical concept of family look like? If we examine the Old Testament, the families described are much more along the lines of what we could call the extended family. There would traditionally be a main household with children and various relatives, and adult children with their families would often live close by. Some displaced persons might also be taken in and become part of the extended family. This provided a much broader, cross-generational conception of family than does our contemporary nuclear family. The Bible speaks of extended families of upward of one hundred members. We are explicitly told

that Abraham's extended family included sixty-six people. This does not mean that we can simply import these details into the contemporary period. But reflecting on these models helps us to see the inadequacy, compared to biblical concepts, of the individualism that is part and parcel of the contemporary "family values" debate. To return to more biblical living, we must begin again to think in much broader communal terms than we usually do in our culture. Our discussion needs to extend well beyond the boundaries of the typical family-values debate if we are to recapture a more Christian way of family and community life.[13]

If people are going to experience the remarkable world of biblical community, they must see connecting as more than just another item to cross off the to-do list. God intends for his followers to make community more than just another activity that occupies their lives. We must embrace it at the core of who we are. The church needs to return to a simpler way and put our hectic schedules on a diet so that we can become all that God intended us to be.

Skepticism

Relationships—you can't live with them; you can't live without them. Each of us will, at some point, be hurt, let down, betrayed, judged, or wounded. Asking people to risk emotional injury is like asking them to commit relational suicide. Their doubts, fears, and hesitations trigger understandable skepticism. Through their tainted lenses we must appear to be charlatans peddling the snake oil of a relational pipe dream.

A few weeks ago, our staff received a staggering email:

I have been putting off this thank-you for months, as
I don't think words could ever adequately express my

gratitude. Last October, I emailed many of you, asking if there was anywhere I could plug in. This last year has been exceptionally difficult, as I feel like I have been shaken to the core. Even though I was very broken and did not have much to offer, you were willing to walk alongside me on the journey. I joined a group. One Sunday, I was asked if we had any prayer requests. My parents are in full-time ministry, and they are struggling relationally, emotionally, physically, and spiritually. I have asked people to pray for them countless times. All that to say, I don't really know why I decided to speak up and ask for prayer for my parents.

To make a long story short, my group surprised me by creating an incredible basket, which included books, CDs, things for Dad and Mom to do together, and a gift certificate for six nights away at the beach! When my Mom and sister walked into the room and saw the basket, my mom started sobbing. She could not believe that a group of people she didn't even know would do something like that for her and Dad. I think we were all speechless. My family will never forget that act of kindness. I want to take this opportunity to let you know that you have impacted my life tremendously. Your demonstration of "faith in action" and genuine desire to enter into relationships with hurting people has helped me to change directions from a wounded skeptic to someone searching for reconciliation and a peace that transcends understanding.

The process of making sense of our wounds is a very personal one. But the most important premise in wound healing is forgiveness. Bitterness leaves us incapable of enjoying healthy relationships. Blame and resentment isolate the soul, but forgiveness helps us reconnect with others.

Skeptics assume the worst in relationships. "I will not be accepted. It will cost me. I won't benefit. I will get hurt. People can't be trusted." They add the sum total of probable outcomes and calculate the risk. Skepticism ultimately is about vision — or lack of it. Skeptics are limited in their ability to look past the inherent negatives, to see beyond the valleys of relational nuisance, and imagine a panorama of exquisite connectedness.

The transition between unplugging and engaging is about overcoming those things that impede our tribal inheritance. What we're experiencing in these breakthrough moments of brushing up against others is God's anthology of a relational dimension. (After writing this, I started to remember a black-and-white image of Rod Serling smoking a cigarette and saying, "You're traveling through another dimension, a dimension not only of sight and sound but of mind. A journey into a wondrous land whose boundaries are that of imagination. That's the sign-post up ahead—your next stop, the Twilight Zone!")

The experience of relational connectedness can be a journey into a wondrous land whose boundaries are that of the imagination. But let's be honest, for many of us this communal dimension freaks us out, asks too much of us, or comes at too great a price. It's a bizarre, strange world for some to grasp. I often meet people who aren't part of a close relational community of believers. Some of them have been burned by past group experiences, and some have overdosed on the chaos and disorder of hectic lives. They find themselves standing on the doorstep of deep relational connectedness, gazing at what could be—only to be restrained by what it might cost. If we are to ever thrive within this communal dimension, we must embrace this realm, regardless of the risk or the price tag. Helping others step into this "our space" domain is what the coffee shop environment is all about; it aims to empower others to take the risk.

This tweener space fixed in the relational journey suspends like a bridge between the solitary sphere of attending and the shared circle of engaging. The merging of these two jurisdictions happens within the "coffee shop" environment as we expose the opportunities for individuals to connect, belong, and engage.

It all starts with exposure. *Your* exposure!

8

polyester suits notwithstanding

Transitioning People

Exposure can be both awkward and amazing. Webster's dictionary describes *expose* in this way: "To cause to be visible or open
to view." It reminds me of Halloween when I was nine years old.
My grandmother was an amazing woman who made life fun for
everyone around her. On this particular Halloween, she invited
the grandkids over to her place to trick-or-treat in her retire-
ment home. (Candy in a denture franchise is, of course, a little
ironic.) I think I was a pirate or the swashbuckling Zorro that
year. Of course, being the fun and entertaining person she was,
Grandma Mae decided to exhibit her own costume—a vintage
Marilyn Monroe outfit. Upon arriving at Grandma Mae's place,
all of us grandkids walked by her dining room table on the way
to her cozy living room. This is where the "awkward" exposure
took place. Taking a side glance, I noticed a set of skin-toned
plastic bosoms sitting in full dual summit on the dining room
table, open to public view. Scarred to this day, I'm not sure
what was more disturbing—the plastic twin-peak mammaries
or the fact that Grandma Mae was making them a part of her

masquerading ensemble. (Now you and I share this image. Misery loves company!)

The hesitation for many in getting connected is the intimidation of community nakedness. They feel the nervous tension developing in their bodies as they hear about transparency, vulnerability, and disclosure. Relational exposure can threaten the stripping down or uncovering of our veiled imperfections. (I love how LifeChurch.tv pastor Craig Groeschel expounds on "fellowship" as "social intercourse.") The intimate shared entwinement that takes place in authentic Christian community can seem X-rated. The whole thing is risqué, and yet it's beautiful. The question is, How do we create exposure to deeper connectedness without it being portrayed like a tasteless spring break video? Here's another way of looking at it: Webster's dictionary also defines *expose* in this way: "to submit or make accessible to a particular action or influence"—the key thought being, *make accessible.*

This type of exposure reminds me of a man named Chris, who attended a men's "coffee shop" event we hosted a couple of years ago. The weekend event had a simple purpose: to create an environment that would give men an opportunity to experience a snapshot of what community feels like. We wanted "to submit or make men accessible to the particular action and influence of *potential relationships.*" This type of relational accessibility would hopefully put them in fraternal proximity. Over the course of the weekend, there were various fun activities, challenges, relevant talks, and, of course, small group breakout sessions.

Chris is a busy guy who is overwhelmed with the typical demands that every man encounters in his daily frenzied world. Over the last few years, he had been attending our Sunday morning "park" environment, but he had now decided to make an attempt at getting connected. Showing up at our men's "coffee shop" event was his next step in that direction. This weekend snapshot of community would only last for a few days—hardly the time needed to experience deep, authentic connection. But it was a glimpse, a taste, a teaser of what could be.

About midway through the weekend, I saw Chris standing in the back of the room with his head down. Only he wasn't alone. Six other men stood with him, arms around each other like they were in a Super Bowl huddle. As I casually walked by, I overheard a couple of the men praying for Chris, salty tears included. They weren't huddled in a football stadium preparing for a championship football game, but Chris had been exposed and made accessible to six new relationships that would champion and cheer for him in his own battles. Later that weekend, Chris shared with me that his wife had just left him and that his entire world was falling apart.

I wish I could tell you that this "coffee shop" weekend had a fairy-tale ending for Chris, but it didn't. All of the prayer, encouragement, and support that he received that weekend didn't result in him riding into the sunset with his wife, the two of them living happily ever after. It did, however, result in Chris connecting with a group of men who to this day walk with him on the other side of divorce.

Chris's encounter that weekend captures the heart behind the "coffee shop" environment. He was exposed to organic relationships that would develop into deeper community connectedness. The success of the "coffee shop" is more than what necessarily happens at the event; it's what happens *after* the event that matters for long-term, sustainable life change. All too often, churches put great effort into events like this but fail to put equal or more time in what the event is intended to lead to. The "coffee shop" events are meant to be a catalyst or temporary context to provide exposure to a sample of what authentic community relationships can look like. It's the place where individuals can experience a taste of their faith intersecting with their real lives. People need accessibility, and it all starts with exposure. Now they can move on to connect, belong, and engage.

Connecting

By giving an individual the opportunity to take the next relational step, it empowers him or her to move through the process toward greater life change. The opposite of movement is a state of dormancy or inactivity. Transition is about *flow*. Consider the example of water. Stagnation occurs when water stops flowing, potentially creating a major environmental hazard. Stagnant water is dangerous to consume because it can be an incubator for all kinds of bacteria and disease. In the same way, churches that do not experience a fresh current often become incubators for bitterness and complacency.

The goal of Grace Chapel's "coffee shop" environment is to help people connect in relationships as quickly as possible. It functions as a temporary step, with the goal of moving someone deeper into more relational experiences. It's about the continual process of moving people from community to community as it inspires them to engage at new levels.

Assimilation is the church-growth word for "closing the back door and helping people connect." Unfortunately, most assimilation methods focus on connecting people to a church vision, strategy, membership, or a program of some sort—rather than connecting them to other amazing people in the church. The danger of assimilation is that it can become a process for generating uniformity rather than leveraging diversity to create community. Our goal is not to make everyone look the same by behaving in the exact same manner. Nor should we simply close the back door to swell our attendance. The aim is to help people discover key relationships. I prefer the word *connect* over *assimilate*. Within our "coffee shop" environment, we seek to help people connect with others in pursuit of authentic biblical community.

The difference between leading a church and leading a movement is the ability to move people into greater relational accountability. The longer people hide in our Sunday services, the easier it is for them to become comfortable blending into the crowd. One of our goals within the "coffee shop" environment is to move people from crowd to conversation. I believe that if we can create an environment where people enter into meaningful conversations, then the Holy Spirit will function like a divine Cupid, supernaturally knitting the right people together.

Motion and connection have to blend together. People may be connecting within the various opportunities that our church provides. Their social calendars are filled with events, conferences, meetings, projects, and volunteering. But are they connecting where and how we want them to connect?

Many people connect just enough to satisfy their need for community. They are content to engage in polite exchanges. We don't have to worry about them leaving due to feeling unwelcome. That's the problem! We want them to engage in a connection that *stimulates motion* toward missional community. In the same vein, people may go through all the motions and participate without experiencing a significant connection.

As we evaluate each "coffee shop" environment, we ask ourselves, "Is it moving people toward where we want them to be?" We want people to move from our "park" environment into our "living room" environment. We define the success of our "coffee shop" environments on the basis of whether or not they empower people to make the transition to a deeper community experience.

We've also discovered that not everyone responds to the transition in the same way or at the same pace. Even though we desire for each person to experience the extraordinary life that is missional community, we understand that it takes more than one dimension of community to help people connect. That's why we offer several opportunities throughout the year and at various seasons—all functioning with the goal of helping people grow and move along the way.

Belonging

People usually experience belonging before they will buy into what you believe. Belonging is not something that happens overnight; it is a process in and of itself—but it has to start somewhere. It's a lot like a blind date. At first you're nervous— your palms are sweaty, you're squirming in your chair and hoping the other person is not some kind of weirdo. But then you discover that each of you likes Cheerios, and now you have something in common to talk about.

At Grace Chapel, creating the sense of belonging that people crave starts in the distinct common spaces we create within the "coffee shop" environments. On the surface, these common spaces may seem unoriginal—and that's because they are. The space may change as we discover new spaces where people experience belonging, but each of them serves the same purpose.

- *Connect Events*. We understand the need to create spaces that allow people to engage within the context of their particular life stage. Whether for men, women, young adults, high schoolers, middle schoolers, parents, or empty nesters—these events are designed to move people from the large crowd of Sunday services to midsize crowds, usually ranging between fifty and one hundred people.

- *Service Projects.* We understand the need to create spaces for people to work side by side, expressing the love of Christ. A special bond transpires among those who forfeit their comfort and absorb the issues that affect the daily lives of others.

- *Focus Groups.* We understand the need to create spaces for people to engage with issues of common relevance. Whether the focus is on financial burdens, grief care, addiction recovery, abuse, boundaries, parenting, or other specific topics—these groups create safe places for people to connect as they face these issues together.

- *Community Groups.* We understand the need to create spaces for people to share in mutual interests. Whether the bond has to do with sports, art, music, recreation, or adventure—these groups create relaxing places for people to enjoy life together.

- *Service Groups.* We understand the need to create spaces for people to practice servanthood toward others. Whether the emphasis is on working with the homeless, helping inmates, greeting guests, or parking cars—these groups create wonderful opportunities for people to assist others. These groups are different from random service projects in that they meet consistently to focus on one aspect of service.

- *LinC Group.* We understand the need to create spaces for people to sample what missional community looks like. LinC ("Living in Community") is a six-week group whose aim is to inspire people to live in a holistic expression of biblical community. These groups facilitate an amazing discovery of our desire for each believer.

- *Global Missions Trips.* We understand the need to create spaces for people to address global issues. Whether the concern is sickness, war, natural disasters, political oppression, or economic subjugation—these excursions create powerful opportunities for people to significantly impact the world.

Once people gain a sense of belonging, it becomes more natural for them to engage.

Engaging

What does it take to get people to engage? It's not about secret formulas, slick campaigns, guilt trips, or gimmicks. (At Grace Chapel we did a series called "Groovy Kind of Love" to inspire people to express love in community. We introduced the theme by lowering a thirty-inch disco ball and playing "Staying Alive" as I walked onto the stage wearing a polyester leisure suit. Sometimes gimmicks can be a starting point, I guess.)

Motion is about calling people to the vision and desperately praying, begging, and hoping that God through his Spirit will supernaturally propel people from sitting to engaging. We leaders have to remember that we cannot call anyone to something we have not lived out in our own lives or something we're not willing to go to our deathbeds modeling. The difference between leading a church and leading a movement is our intentionality about moving people from attendance to engagement. Here are four crucial aspects to motion.

Opportunity

Moving people from attendance to engagement means giving them opportunities to connect. These opportunities function like on-ramps joining two paths. They empower people to join the process from wherever they are on their spiritual journey.

It's only an opportunity if it actually works for the person it's intended for. The vision may be to see people engage at "stage ten" of community, but for those who are at stage one or two, the leap is too big. Opportunities for connection need to come with clear, simple next steps. Each opportunity should aim toward moving people one step forward from wherever they are.

Timing

People typically don't respond well to pressure. They do not want to feel manipulated or forced into something they're not ready for. I understand the importance of stretching people beyond what they think they can handle, but I've also come to realize that there are seasons to life. I have made the mistake of pushing people into something prematurely, and as a result, I did not set them up to succeed.

People move through their spiritual journey at different paces. One person's pace is not better than another's. Often, outside circumstances determine the speed of someone's progress along the discipleship process. It is critical to allow people to have ongoing windows of opportunities throughout the year to engage when timing is in their favor. Our windows of engagement should be in rhythm with their windows of opportunity.

Trust

As the cliché goes, it takes time to build trust. If we are going to help people move from attendance to engagement, then we have to be intentional about letting them experience a taste of what could be. Even God presented this kind of offer: "Taste and see that the LORD is good" (Psalm 34:8).

People are going to have to trust that what "we want" for them is what "they think" is best for them as well. This happens only as they grow confident in our willingness to listen and seek to understand them. Without this, we come across as phony. It's essential for them to understand that we are not calling them to a program, an event, or a project; we are calling them to Jesus.

Relationship

People respond to people. Nothing compares to a personal invitation to participate in relationship. I am regularly approached by wives in our church who beg me to extend a personal invitation to their husbands: "If you ask him, I know he will engage." They are right. In the busyness of church life, we can never overlook the critical influence of personal interaction. This past week, I was sitting in my office when I took a phone call. On the other end of the line, a fragile voice pleaded, "Mike, I need help. I think I'm going to leave him." She went on to explain the escalading tone of her husband's angry vernacular directed at her, including the repetitive use of "shut up" and "bitch." Her request was direct and genuine. "Please get him plugged into a group of men who can help him. He looks up to you and will go if you invite him."

No matter how motivated, creative, intentional, or theological we are, people will always engage more naturally through the tangible expression of organic relationships. Relationship is the natural link that moves people from attendance to engagement. A warm expression of genuine connectivity is powerful.

Because of the power of relationships, Grace Chapel has been intentional about putting people face-to-face. Twice a year, we ask our small group leaders to attend all of our weekend services. In each of these services, we create the space for guests to meet them. We cut our services to half of our normal meeting time and explain that the rest of the time will be devoted to giving people the opportunity to mingle in the room and connect.

It's not the only thing we do—and it certainly is not a guarantee that everyone will make a connection. But it creates a highly relational environment where people can initiate conversations. These "connecting Sundays" have become a significant catalyst for the Holy Spirit to attach people together. When the Holy Spirit orchestrates a collage of seemingly random lives, a portrait of divine beauty surfaces.

Faith in real life isn't just about connecting people; it's about *why* we are connecting them. The "coffee shop" environment is about moving people to the ultimate journey of doing life together within the context of missional community as they live out a shared expression of following Jesus. This past Sunday, instead of delivering a potentially redundant message about biblical community, I decided to illustrate it from the platform—live. Black leather couches, a rug, and an end table were arranged into a living room motif. Sitting on the couches were five individuals plus myself.

Like a talk show host in front of a live studio audience, I facilitated an open discussion. It was full disclosure, representing the stories of lives being changed through our "living room" environment. Moving from person to person, I posed this question: "How has being in community changed your life?" In response, David and Barbara, sitting on the far left, openly shared about the devastation of their previous divorces. Then

Kit and Clay, a young married couple sitting in the middle, walked us through their journey of infertility and the struggle to begin a family. Finally, to my immediate right sat Tara, a young single mom, who took us into her world of abuse and abandonment.

That Sunday morning, the crowd was impressed. No, they were actually more than impressed. They were inspired by the genuineness and honest admission of these five people, who did more that just divulge their concealed circumstances; they expressed how their community lovingly walked with them through their valleys.

If you think this was a brilliant way to illustrate authenticity and care, it would only be partly true. Beyond sharing about the context in which they received communal care, these folks expounded on being part of something that was bigger than a support group. They gave us a glimpse into what their groups were doing to impact the world—things such as serving the poor together, addressing poverty together, and loving the untouchable together. They opened the door into their missional community. They invited us into their "living room" environment. It's the threshold we now cross over to enter.

Part 4

the living room

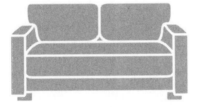

9

fire in the house

Building Relationships

As I was growing up in the 1970s, our living room looked like something out of the set of the *Brady Bunch*. Orangeish faux fur couches, gold floral wallpaper, and a wood-paneled TV set that must have weighed five hundred pounds. Today our TVs have gotten flatter, and our couches have become, well, less fuzzy. Regardless of the decor makeovers that have transpired within our dwellings, our living rooms are choreographed for maximum comfort and entertainment.

Today, the elements of a modern living room may include a high-def TV, surround sound speakers, a wireless Internet connection, leather sectional sofas, and an interactive gaming system. Even though these components are primarily designed to add to the personal stimulation of our habitat, the social function of the living room still remains. Whether you're into contemporary, English country, Victorian, or vintage retro design, your living room is a natural setting for intimacy and shared existence.

In a culture where amusement and leisure are increasingly fundamental to our lives, the interior of a home may reflect the pursuit of social goals and symbolize the personal status of its occupant.

Ironically, our living rooms feed our voyeuristic appetites by serving as portals into the private living rooms of notorious celebrities. Our obsession with reality TV shows can arouse our desire to be invited into the most personal of spaces.

Come On In

Being personally invited into someone's home feels elevating. Our homes express who we are. They reveal the food we like to eat, the music we listen to, the art we admire, the books we read, and the things we spend our money on. When guests arrive, we indulge their curiosity by embarking on our own version of MTV's *Cribs*. These courteous room-by-room tours uncover more than just our hospitality; they reveal our need to know and be known.

Being invited into someone's living room is a gesture of acceptance and approval that says to you, "I trust you and enjoy spending time with you enough that I am willing to share more of my life with you."

Consider two friends who have met regularly over coffee, and now one invites the other over for dinner. It suggests a natural progression of intimacy and value. It's the logical (and expected) next step. To continue meeting only in the coffee shop would limit the potential for a deeper relationship.

Even our postures within the living room can suggest various degrees of intimacy. From sitting on the couch to lying on the floor, each position evokes the comfortableness of the relationship. Perhaps the greatest expression connected to being invited into someone's home is the prevailing sense that you are considered like family to your hosts. In fact, some people refer to their living room as "the family room." It's a safe place to open your heart, share your life, and ask tough questions. It's about commitment, strength, and love. It's not only about having a space to be yourself; it's about having others walk alongside of you—people who are committed to your potential and your welfare.

The metaphor of the living room is perfect for describing relational intimacy. As Jesus used parables to illustrate spiritual truth, we use the living room as a parable to illustrate the concept of *belonging to the family of God*. Everything about the living room says "family"—from the geeky family portrait on the wall to the trinkets on the mantel from last summer's vacation.

At Grace Chapel, the image of the living room represents our desire to see every person thriving in holistic community. The strategic process of moving people from "community to community" culminates in this environment. Because we see church as a process instead of an event, we understand that it must develop a thread of relationships.

Our desire is to effectively communicate, inspire, and lead every person into the most relational environment possible. An environment that fosters relationship must be one that promotes safety, enables people to relax, and makes them feel as though they can be themselves. Therefore, we don't offer Sunday school classes because we want to see our people in an environment where they can kick off their shoes, recline on the floor, munch on food, lounge on the couch, or even curl up in a blanket—and you just can't do that in a sterile setting.

It is important to note that the living room is our relational destination, not our spiritual destination. We are aiming for life change—being transformed into the image of Jesus Christ. That is a lifelong journey. Our strategy is to get people into the most relationally conducive environment in order to maximize the opportunity for life change.

We understand that without specific direction, people will not naturally end up where we want them. People need destinations. Left without guidance, they will roam, aimlessly searching for what you already know they need. Sheep need to be told by their shepherds where to find the finest pasture that will satisfy their hunger.

If a church strategy is going to be intentional at forming relationships, it needs a relational metaphor as its philosophy of ministry—relationship with God, relationship with the world, and relationship with each other.

Grab a Bite to Eat

My wife loves to bake—and I love to eat any baked item that materializes out of her culinary genius. In the vast pantheon of her baking brilliance, nothing compares to the mouthwatering explosion of flavor that is her Indian fry bread fajitas. Her recipe is a prized family heirloom, passed down from the greatness of the dough gods themselves. It takes hours of preparation to master the fry bread, but it's worth it.

Now imagine trying to get the same experience from eating individual ingredients of the fry bread—the flour, baking powder, yeast, salt, oil, and honey. Instead of experiencing the beauty of all the ingredients coming together in an amazing blend of perfection, you taste only the reduced flavor of the fry bread's parts.

Reductionism originated during the Enlightenment. It was a product of modernity and the corresponding belief that knowledge is best discovered through the scientific method. Not only did reductionism become established as one of society's great achievements; it found its way into the church too. The bride of Christ became a picture of disintegration. Instead of having individual parts add to the whole, the parts become the isolated personality disorders within the body.

Compartmentalizing is hazardous to our spiritual health. It is the means by which we reduce our understanding of spirituality into microcosms. Think about it—people are always defining spirituality by just a few aspects of spiritual expression (usually those that complement their own particular spiritual gifting). For some, it's prayer. You hear them say, "If we just prayed more, we could ..." For some, it's studying the Word. You hear them say, "If we just studied God's Word more, we could ..." For others, it's the Holy Spirit. You hear them say, "If only we had more of the Spirit, we could ..." You get the idea. Usually we end up lobbying for our personal agendas to make the church primarily about our one thing. Somehow, it's easy to believe that by embracing just one of these aspects, we will achieve the pinnacle of spiritual enlightenment.

A lot of tension results from our reductionist approach— our tendency to put God in a box. But amid the turmoil, a worldview is emerging that paints a different picture to describe spirituality and our journey with Christ; it's a picture of all the ingredients coming together. People with this worldview prefer the taste of fry bread to the taste of its individual parts.

When all of the parts come together, divine synergy propels the church forward. Holistic community is not just about connecting; it's about creating space for all aspects of spiritual development to thrive. It's not just another aspect of spiritual development; it's a way of life.

The greatest opportunity for sustainable life change is when intentional relationships are formed within the context of community. Of course, not *any* type of community will lead to a life-changing experience. This environment has to be more than just connecting or studying the Bible; it has to be about living, breathing, and interacting with Scripture. Holistic community is about joining a group of followers who actively live out their faith in an all-encompassing way.

The word *holistic* may conjure up for you an association with alternative medicine or the picture of a scruffy bearded guy sitting in the lotus position. Before you draw the conclusion that I am some hippie New Age maharishi wannabe pastor, let me suggest that holistic community is what God intended for us to experience. *Holism* originates from the Greek word *holos*, which means "all," "entire," "total." It is the idea that all the properties of a given system cannot be determined or explained by its component parts alone. Instead, the system as a whole determines in an important way how the parts behave.

Holism within the Bible refers to the wholeness of the person. When it comes to the life change that so many of us are championing, holism is concerned with the qualitative spiritual development of the whole person, both as an individual and as part of a community.

Holistic community highlights the identity of its various parts by relating them to the whole and recognizing their inseparable nature. Holistic community allows us to discover our identity in Christ as all the parts come together to find mutual significance. The apostle Paul affirms this in his letter to the Romans: "Just as each of us has one body with many members, and these members do not all have the same function, so in Christ we, though many, form one body, and each member belongs to all the others" (Romans 12:4 – 5).

Common ground is the yeast of communities. It's what encourages the rise of spiritual development. It creates a place where the divine word of God can meet with the power of the Holy Spirit. This common ground reveals the redemptive power of the gospel as it unites the wholeness of spirituality with the wholeness of the person. It's about completion.

Tell Me Your Story

Each year, the small group Bernadette and I belong to holds a Christmas party. One year, after a vigorous online forum discussing party themes, we opted for the traditional white elephant gift exchange—a swap of unwanted items and regifted atrocities. Often a few good items are thrown in the mix too, making the gift exchange more fun. Spread across the living room floor were the unusual presents we'd merrily wrapped and were eager to reveal: a gift card, oven mitts, a *High School Musical* poster, a lottery ticket, a set of novelty drinking glasses, and so on. Among the tattered pile of wrappings was a gift of great value: a large picture frame holding a collection of photos that captured special moments we had shared as a group. It was a visual history of camping trips, birthday parties, dinners, and travels together—a celebration of lives that were divinely connected into relational cohesion.

I went home that night with this prized possession, which now hangs on my wall in my office—reminding me of what community really looks like.

Sharing our stories can help us understand ourselves and others. It's a powerful way of processing individual experiences. Every person is part of a story. Pulling back the curtain of eternity will reveal that all of these stories became interconnected into one scripted narrative of divine correlation.

In his book *An Unstoppable Force*, Erwin McManus enlightens us on the art of story:

Apostolic leaders are great storytellers, and they make sure that the great story is central in shaping the ethos of the community. . . .

The church was born out of stories. The first-century church was driven by the narrative. There was no New Testament; there were no Gospels to transmit the story of Jesus. His story was entrusted to storytellers. The Christian faith grew through story—not text. Only later did the stories become Scripture. While the Scripture must be held in the highest regard, we must not neglect the power of story.[14]

The essence of story begins with the essence of God, as seen in the origins of humanity's relationship with him. In creating human beings, God hinted at the connection between Father, Son, and Holy Spirit: "Then God said, 'Let us make human beings in our image, in our likeness'" (Genesis 1:26).

The remarkable expression of plurality in "us" and "our" sets the stage for our understanding of God. Within the communal framework of the triune God are three distinct beings perfectly rendered as one unified entity—which, as Bill Donahue and Russ Robinson explain, reveals that "it is not enough to say God is interested in community or even obsessed with community. God, rightly defined and understood, *is* community."[15]

A significant part of telling the creation story means living within the context of community. As image bearers of God, our destiny is woven into the fabric of shared existence. Our souls were created to be the characters within the anecdote of heaven's storybook. As the Son of Man walked with his community of disciples, he imparted this truth: "Where two or three come together in my name, there am I with them" (Matthew 18:20). As mutual characters in this sublime novel, we stand as mirrors that reflect back between each other the romantic interface of a perfect protagonist, Jesus Christ.

When we step into community, we step into God's redemptive story — a masterpiece that begins with our genesis and continues into eternity. Many people think that their spiritual journey is intended to be a biographical sketch of solitude. They pontificate on the notion of solitude with God in a mystical sort of way. I'm all for one's quiet time with God. We can light candles, meditate on sacred Scriptures, pen poems, and sing along with Chris Tomlin CDs. However, living like monks in a cave is not the chapter of our lives that God wants to write about. Since God exists within community, works within community, and created us to experience him through community, our story of being in community is the portrait that hangs on the wall, identifying us as the family of God. The canon of Scripture is closed, but the story of human beings living in community with God and with each other is still being written.

We have to help people recover from the tendency to think like deists. Deism is the worldview that says God created the world and then stood back to watch. Deism pictures God as uninvolved. It denies the inspiration of the Bible, the incarnation of Jesus Christ, and the reality of miracles or any other supernatural behavior on God's part. But the Bible is not a fairy tale, fable, or folklore. It is the story of God intervening so that human beings can live out their lives in the image of their Creator.

Our personal story makes sense only when conveyed in the context of the whole story. Imagine reading a script in which you are given the lines from just one character. The story would be incomprehensible. It's the symbiotic dialogue among characters that reveals the plot. This great story is full of subplots with related themes: sagas of reconciled relationships, restored marriages, emotional healing, compassionate care, and sin that has been overcome. It all happens in the context of God creating us to live in his image—together.

All Together Now

Last year was an interesting one for our small group. We've been journeying together for more than three years now. Our group is diverse—which is why I love each person. Some are sweet, and some are spicy! With this blend of personalities, things can get a little stirred up at times. Early in our communal experience, I remember having a remarkable dialogue. Sitting on the living room floor, we began to see ourselves as a group of friends who would journey together with the purpose of discovering the fullness of Christ through one another. We validated each other's distinct giftings, passions, life experiences, and abilities. Our goal was to support each other in our exploration of our gifting. We recognized that at times the expression of our gifts would stretch us and provoke us to do things we would never do alone—and that this might make us uncomfortable. But it wasn't about compatibility or personal comfort; it was about complementing each other and allowing the Spirit of God to show himself through us.

Independence is the sign of immaturity; interdependence is the sign of growth. For example, I personally do not have the gift of compassion. It's not my natural desire to wake up every morning and hang out with the homeless under an overpass. I need others in my group who have the gift of compassion to reveal it to me. One person with compassion inspires us to see an opportunity and reach out to the homeless. One person with administrative gifts organizes an outreach evening. Another with the gift of help prepares food to hand out. Another with the gift of intercession bathes the experience in prayer. Another with the gift of hospitality opens his or her home to invite the homeless off the streets. Together we become a more complete representation of Christ to each other and to the world.

This mutually advantageous joining of distinct elements is captured by Paul in his letter to the Corinthians:

> There are different kinds of gifts, but the same Spirit distributes them. There are different kinds of service, but the same Lord. There are different kinds of working, but in all of them and in everyone it is the same God at work.
>
> Now to each one the manifestation of the Spirit is given for the common good.
>
> 1 CORINTHIANS 12:4–7

In response to a letter from one of the members of the church at Corinth, Paul had to lay down the law. Many church members were trying to hustle their way into positions of importance by suggesting that their gifts were more important than other people's gifts. Their posturing was the opposite of what God intended with regard to their spiritual gifts. These extraordinary gifts from the Holy Spirit were meant to bless and build up the community of faith, not to make people feel inferior.

Paul explained that the manifestation of the Spirit is given *for the common good*. The Greek word for *common* is *koinos*, which denotes "belonging to the group," not to the individual. It's also the root word for *koinonia*, a rich and complex word for "community."

The early Christian community made no distinction between their relationships with each other and with God. One aspect of *koinonia* was that Christian community was about more than belonging; it was also about embracing and promoting that which benefits the greater good of the whole. A related Greek word, *enthousiasmos* (from which the English word *enthusiasm* is derived), suggests the idea of "God in us" (*en* + *theos*, "inspired by God").

When we think of *enthusiasm*, we tend to picture someone with passion, fervor, or zeal. It may, for instance, conjure up an image of a flamboyant, curly-haired physical fitness expert who likes to wear tight-fitting short shorts and claps and shouts a lot. (Just admit it, you once owned a pair of those candy-striped Dolfin shorts.) Enthusiasm conveys life and vibrancy as a result of being filled with God. The early Christian community understood that when God infuses someone with a special gifting, the expression of that gift should create a sense of life and vibrancy among the whole community.

Synergy is what happens when followers of Jesus express their gifting within the context of community. God did not intend for our gifts to waste away in isolation; he intended them to complement each other.

The incredible synergy generated among a small group of believers who embrace their uniqueness leads to a symphony of splendor, a concerto of instruments united to produce sounds that no single instrument could create by itself, a sort of communal opus. Community is the theatrical stage where the performance of the Spirit of God can portray the masterpiece of his finely tuned craftsmanship, his church. Brian McLaren captures this point in his book *The Story We Find Ourselves In*:

> A violin master is someone who can take an instrument of wood and wire and horsehair and play it so that it yields music more beautiful than anyone else can play. And for the disciples to call Jesus "master" would mean ... yes, it would mean that no one else could take the raw materials

of life—skin and bone and blood and space and time and words and deeds and waking and sleeping and eating and walking—and elicit from them a beautiful song of truth and goodness, as Jesus did.[16]

Time for Fireworks

When I was a kid, I loved to play with fire. Something about its ominous glow mesmerized me. (OK, not just when I was a kid. I still have a little pyromania in me.) I remember one fantastic summer day when I was in the seventh grade. My family was moving from Southern California to western Canada. For a thirteen-year-old boy, it was a summer that created lasting memories. It was only days before Independence Day. As we made our way up the I–5 corridor through Portland, my younger brother Jason and I stocked up on our personal stashes of pyrotechnics. Every gas station, grocery store, or roadside stand promised a new assortment of dangerous delights. We could not resist our most primal of desires—blowing things up. Who could pass up the opportunity to launch something called "Explodimus Maximus" or "The Big No-No"?

In keen anticipation, we envisioned a display of explosive magnificence. We devised a plan to light them at a nearby marina on the Columbia River. The well-mortared dock bordered by water would surely provide a safe zone for detonation. Approaching the end of the dock, we cautiously set down our bag of firecrackers, pinwheels, sparklers, and rockets. Carefully we selected one item at a time and began to set them off with delight. Each multihued explosion seduced us into enchantment.

A few minutes into our celebration, my brother ignited a bottle rocket. As it took its fiery course through the sky, it aimed its flight path back toward the dock, landing directly in his bag of fireworks. The aftermath was a spectacular display of chaos. With only a few feet to maneuver on the edge of the dock, we were bombarded with the anarchy of gunpowder and phosphorus.

All this to say, community is the commitment to ignite the church into a spontaneous and spectacular display of spiritual combustion.

Combustion happens when fuel and oxidants react. Oxidants are compounds that readily transfer oxygen. You don't have to be Mr. Wizard to understand that fire needs oxygen in order to burn; it's a principle we've all come to understand as we learned to make campfires. Community is not the fuel or the fire; the Holy Spirit is. The metaphor of the Holy Spirit as fire is a perfect symbol for warmth, light, purification, and heat. Consider Acts 2:3: "[The apostles] saw what seemed to be tongues of fire that separated and came to rest on each of them."

We see that the Holy Spirit is associated with fire in the words of John the Baptist in Matthew 3:11: "I baptize you with water for repentance. But after me comes one who is more powerful than I, whose sandals I am not worthy to carry. He will baptize you with the Holy Spirit and fire."

Community provides the space for the Holy Spirit to infuse with oxygen. Community gives people a place to breathe and sort out what the Holy Spirit is doing in their lives. Remember the story of the Coloumbes, the couple that wanted to reach out to the homeless community? That was just a spark; but the Holy Spirit blew it into a full flame, leading them to sell their possessions and travel the nation in an RV, loving the homeless. Our small group gave them room to breathe and figure out what their calling might look like. They never had all the answers, and neither did we; but we listened, encouraged, exhorted, and experimented along with them. It was a holy process of fanning the flame of God's Spirit already at work in them.

Countless times someone in our group has shared an idea, thought, or feeling that they believe the Holy Spirit may have given them. We see ourselves as providing the best place to let these ideas or feelings breathe. In fact, this book is a direct result of what I have experienced with them and what the Holy Spirit has put on my heart.

Our churches are full of people who are prompted by the Holy Spirit to engage in amazing things. They only need a place to breathe and process what God is doing in their lives. In other words, our churches are full of Andys and Serenitys. Imagine a church that explodes in brilliance as its people are given the right environment—oxygen for the spark of flame that the Holy Spirit has ignited within them. I dream about this every day!

People discover the truth of their conviction not simply through reason but primarily through experience and participation. Reason is still valued, but it needs to be connected to an experience in which they can engage. Community provides the harmony between being knowledge based and experience based.

I think of the heartening words that Paul expressed to the Philippian community:

> Therefore, my dear friends, as you have always obeyed—not only in my presence, but now much more in my absence—continue to work out your salvation with fear and trembling, for it is God who works in you to will and to act in order to fulfill his good purpose.
>
> PHILIPPIANS 2:12–13

Community needs to be a place to work out our salvation, a place to struggle through and move forward. Community needs to be a safe place to experiment with fire. By *safe*, I don't mean controlled, but gracious and patient. I think the word *experiment* is a good one for describing our response to God in community. Experimenting demands risk. Its goal is to discover a major breakthrough. Discovering one's spiritual gift cannot be done through inventory tests or well-defined listings alone. Usually it starts with a desire or passion and is confirmed by others as they observe God at work in your life. By empowering someone to discover and live out his or her gifting through a community, the whole church is unleashed.

Is your faith on a leash?

10

turtles with their necks out

Going Deeper

Living in the heart of a trendy urban settlement such as downtown Portland can be exciting and fascinating, especially with some of its more bizarre expressions of society. The former industrial section of northwest Portland has morphed into a thriving community of artists' lofts, urban parks, kitsch galleries, and restaurants. Bernadette and I fell in love with its gritty cosmopolitan landscape.

Shortly after setting up residence there, I agreed to participate in a men's retreat hosted at a camp located outside of Portland in a small town called Canby. During one of the afternoon free sessions, I decided to check out Canby.

My tour must have lasted no more than ten minutes. For a city dweller like me, Canby had me seeing a Mayberry knock-off. All that was missing was Barney Fife. Without thinking, I was waving to all oncoming traffic, and I began to have a hankering for a loose-fitting, one-piece work garment known as a "coverall." As I was driving out of town I made a statement out loud as I surveyed the hee-haw hickishness of this not so urban town: "I would never want to live here." And that's exactly how I felt in that moment, followed strangely by a sense that I had just induced the ironic humor of God. My conscience haunted me. Something inside of me realized I had sealed my fate and was destined to become a resident of this rural settlement.

It happened just three years later when I accepted my position at Grace Chapel. And much to my surprise, this tranquil little town—which is actually a large suburban town with several stoplights and a plethora of fast-food chains—has provided some of the most rousing community experiences in my life.

The small group to which my family belongs includes seven couples and nineteen kids who range from newborns to middle schoolers. We go camping together; attend our kids' games together; coach sports teams together; go on mission trips together; see movies, feed the homeless, and celebrate holidays and birthdays together; serve in the church, take vacations, share meals together, and more. In addition to our entire group's weekly gatherings, the guys get together Friday mornings at a local greasy spoon.

This is my community.

Part of a Mosaic

Recently a couple at Grace Chapel and I were discussing their small group. After a few moments, the man whispered, "You know, our group is a little challenging. We have a lot of messed-up people in there." Of course there are messed-up people in our groups! And we're probably one of them. God envisioned community as the place where we would comprehend his mercy and grace. To know and be known means belonging to a community of friends who look past our unpleasant features and see a beautiful individual created in the image of God. By *belong*, I refer to the loving and grace-filled acceptance of those who may appear different or deficient.

I remember one Sunday when Bernadette and I were living in downtown Portland. We invited any new people who had visited our church that day to join us after the service for a barbecue lunch at our home. It was a casual affair with a buffet line in the dining room.

Most of the people were pretty normal. But I noticed someone leaning against the wall. I could tell everyone had taken notice of his presence. His skin was covered in flaky rashes and scabby lesions; it looked a lot like how I imagined leprosy to look. As he joined the buffet line, his peeling hands reached over the food, just as everyone else's did.

As uncomfortable as it made me feel, it was also beautiful to see him welcomed, accepted, and valued by our community. He materialized from invisible to visible. I couldn't help but become aware that his outer shell did not compare to the wretchedness of my inner self-centeredness. I found out later that someone from our small group had invited him to join us at the barbecue — and by so doing, they had enabled me to experience a greater understanding of what the kingdom of God looks like.

Community is meant to be an earthly space for expressing the kingdom of God in us. Essential to this royal realm is an upside-down economy where the first are last and the "least of these" are cherished.

What if Jesus had spent time only with the rich and powerful or the brilliant and beautiful? What portrait of him would we have? The reality is that Jesus gathered a community of people who had been marginalized and rejected — and from that community created a beautiful mosaic. The people Jesus surrounded himself with had broken, messy lives bonded together by his grace, acceptance, and love. These are the mosaics that hang in the eternal gallery, on display for the world to see. Those who reclaim the vision to embrace that which is messy will end up being conduits of a love and grace that will illuminate the world.

The apostle John recorded a revolutionary statement of identity made by Jesus to his followers: "A new command I give you: Love one another. As I have loved you, so you must love one another. By this everyone will know that you are my disciples, if you love one another" (John 13:34–35).

A new command? The imperative to love one another was not original, but to have a type of love that was modeled by Jesus was. To put this rare expression of love in perspective consider the historical background given by Joseph H. Mayfield, a professor of philosophy and New Testament Greek:

> Our Lord's love reached to a Judas who would betray Him, and a Peter who would deny Him. In fact this kind of love was an event so unique that a new verbal vehicle had to be devised to express it. The *eros* of the Greeks described only selfish love; and *philia* described no more than the friendship love that thinks in terms of getting as well as giving. But the selfless sacrifice of Jesus, His willingness to give all without any guarantee of human response, had to be expressed in a stronger word. So *agape*, a rare word for love prior to Paul, came to be used in early Christian literature to describe the kind of love that Jesus demonstrated, and the quality of love that is to characterize the lives of His true disciples.[17]

The endorsement of the church would be on the basis for determining whether Jesus' followers loved one another in the way he demonstrated. The character of his love was demonstrated by his selflessness. The context of his love was community. Together, the character and context of his love are what set the Christian community apart. This divine, majestic way of *agape* love prompts the onlooker to exclaim with wonder, "Look at how these Christ-followers relate. I have never seen an expression of love like this anywhere."

Looking deep into the church, many see only hypocrisy, judgmentalism, anger, selfishness, greed, and pride. For many, the church has blood on its hands. The love that Jesus identified as the defining mark of his true followers often seems to be missing. Is it extinct? No. It's buried in the rubble of broken and shattered existence. Community digs that go beneath the surface of shallow interactions excavate transcendent love and lead to the discovery of rare pigments of beauty embedded within the fragmented textiles of our lives.

Why is a mosaic the perfect image for defining what it means to belong to a community of Christ-followers? Because the Master Artist provided this context for the broken, wretched fragments of our souls to be fitted into a divine mural portraying the image of grace, forgiveness, mercy, compassion, patience, long-suffering, and devotion. It is the image of one individual carrying the burden of another. It's not just about connecting; it's about belonging and finding our place in the redemptive picture. In her book *Community That Is Christian*, Julie Gorman reflects, "We should not think of love as the cause of relatedness. We are already related whether we like it or not. What love does is redeem our relatedness."[18]

Visible

If you're a superhero, having the power to become invisible is cool; if you're a Christian, becoming invisible is tempting. We don't like it when others see our mess. We have junk drawers and closets in which to hide the disarray of our lives. We tend to sweep things under the carpet, covering our personal failures with a facade of pretense. But to live this way deprives us of the opportunity to live out God's purpose.

Community is the audience where the dark hidden secrets of my depravity face the revealing power of grace and intimacy. Community replaces shameful denial and rejection with approval and embrace. It gives purpose and meaning to my own jagged misery. Consider Paul's explanation to suffering Corinthian believers:

> All praise to the God and Father of our Master, Jesus the Messiah! Father of all mercy! God of all healing counsel! He comes alongside us when we go through hard times, and before you know it, he brings us alongside someone else who is going through hard times so that we can be there for that person just as God was there for us.
>
> 2 CORINTHIANS 1:3 – 5 MSG

The first night our small group met together, I opened with a straightforward question that surprisingly went deep for those in the room. "How would you like to see God use this group to change your life?"

Usually when such personal questions are asked at the very first meeting of a small group, people zip up and shrink back like frightened turtles. That night was an extraordinary experience — one that turned out quite differently from the way I expected it to turn out. After the question hung there in silence for a minute or two, one of the guys confessed, "I struggle with sexual addiction."

It was full disclosure, a magical recollection that helped everyone else in the group find their own voice.

Impressed by such transparency, someone else vaulted out of his chair and shouted, "That's what I'm talking about! That's the type of authentic group I want to be a part of!"

He expressed it for all of us. One by one, each of us continued to unpack our suitcases of personal hang-ups.

I am sure that we all went home that night wondering if we had said too much, or if any of our personal exposé would lead to shunning. The following week, we processed the experience and affirmed the openness we had found at our first meeting. Everyone was quick to insist that grace, love, and honesty would provide the bedrock on which we would build our group. Since then, every piece of openness has been welcomed, embraced, and appreciated. Our attitude of belonging and acceptance can be traced back to that very first evening we shared as a group.

A few days ago, I was talking with my neighbor on his front porch. Bill is the guy I mentioned earlier—the one who wears tattoos like sleeves on both arms. Bill had never been to church and was wondering if he should cover up his well-inked arms before coming in. "Absolutely not!" I exclaimed. I did not want Bill's first experience with church to begin with an act of covering up. The community of Jesus Christ is about being exposed and then encountering the loving embrace of God's kingdom.

It makes me think of the story of Zacchaeus—the wealthy tax collector hated by the common people. He was also a little man. As Jesus passed through Jericho, Zacchaeus climbed a tree in order to see him better. When Jesus reached that spot, he looked up at the branches, addressed Zacchaeus by name, and told him to come down. Then Jesus invited himself over for dinner. The crowd was shocked: "All the people saw this and began to mutter, 'He has gone to be the guest of a sinner'" (Luke 19:7).

I often wonder if Zacchaeus climbed that tree not just to catch a glimpse of Jesus but with the hope that Jesus would catch a glimpse of him. Deep down, we all want people to know our story, our pain, our desires. Jesus made no distinction or boundaries between thieves, whores, murderers, or scoundrels. The deep-rooted longing to be visible and to belong is something we all share. Unconditional love is always the first step toward authentic biblical community — the place in which radical grace can thrive in the reflection of Jesus Christ. I composed a short inventory of what this place would look like in an effort to wrap my mind around its tangible expression.

- a place where you are accepted for who you really are
- a place where you are loved unconditionally
- a place where you are listened to — really listened to
- a place where you can share the desires of your heart without criticism
- a place where you can share your fears without being made fun of
- a place where you can discuss the struggles of everyday life
- a place where you can confess without being judged
- a place where someone will celebrate your victories

Going Vintage

A friend of mine once asked one of the most profound questions I've ever heard: "How much community is enough?" The answer is complicated. And the ancient church's perspective would almost certainly be different from ours. The first followers of Jesus modeled the closest expression of community that Jesus intended for us. For them, community was not a program or some forty-day event. It was a lifestyle—a way of doing life—and they were known for it.

A part of me would rather not know what the church is known for today. My guess is we are still known as "the way"— but in terms of the way we judge, the way we boast, the way we exclude. The early church, however, was known for a way of life that expressed the love of Jesus within the context of community. Christ-followers were known for their revolutionary lifestyle that stood out as a wondrous expression of belonging. Reflect on these powerful illustrations.

> All the believers were together and had everything in common. They sold property and possessions to give to anyone who had need.
>
> ACTS 2:44–45

> All the believers were one in heart and mind. No one claimed that any of their possessions was their own, but they shared everything they had.
>
> ACTS 4:32

> In the midst of a very severe trial, their overflowing joy and their extreme poverty welled up in rich generosity. For I testify that they gave as much as they were able, and even beyond their ability. Entirely on their own, they urgently pleaded with us for the privilege of sharing in this service to the Lord's people.
>
> 2 CORINTHIANS 8:2–4

Jesus' disciples took him seriously when he said, "Love each other as I have loved you" (John 15:12). Belonging has to be about a shared life experience, not a shared group meeting. When we take a casual approach to community, we walk away with an impotent, dysfunctional understanding of community. True community is more than just showing up at someone's house and eating casseroles. It's more than finger food and giggles. A person will not experience true belonging or authentic New Testament community by sporadically attending a group. It's not about checking something off a to-do list, thus making it about as important as getting an oil change or picking up the clothes from the dry cleaner.

Belonging involves sharing. Sharing is more than showing up, although that's where it starts. I often hear someone say, "I'm just not getting anything out of our group," or, "I'm just not connecting with the others in our group." Whenever I hear these comments, I ask, "What are you putting in to it?" Usually, you only get out of community life what you put in to it. Belonging will cost us something. It takes effort and sacrifice. It usually requires aligning our lives around our small group as a main entrée, not a side dish.

When people ask me about our groups at Grace Chapel and why we experience belonging and shared intimacy, my response has a nostalgic flavor: we've gone back to the vintage style of community experienced by the first followers of Jesus, as embodied by the following principles.

- *Priority over plurality.* Because our culture moves at a hectic pace, community easily slips down the list of our priorities. Making community a priority affirms its essential place in our lives. If it's a priority, then it's more than just a meeting; it gets our time and commitment.

- *Public over private. Private* means I come to the group but never really share my own story or struggles. *Public* means I share my life with others. Being public empowers others to move beyond just showing up; it frees them to participate in the act of sharing hurts, pain, insecurities, dreams, and ambitions. A willingness to divulge the most personal issues will increase the sense of intimacy within the group, creating even more opportunity for members to minister to and edify one another. Transparency keeps the group from being stifled and stagnated.

- *Others over self.* People often join groups for what they can get out of them. Being selfless removes the pressure for groups to cater to my expectations. Selflessness moves people to see their participation as an opportunity to impact someone else. They are there to be God's instrument—his conduit of love into the soul of another. Ironically, joining a group to minister to others will transpire as the most rewarding thing a person can do for themselves.

- *Missional focus over inward focus.* Serving together revitalizes the energy of a group. The value of being cause oriented is greater than the value of individual comfort. Connecting to a group that champions a cause serves as an outward expression of love to a hurting culture and has long-lasting effects.

- *State of being over state of doing. State of doing* focuses on the group's activities, whereas *state of being* focuses on its character. *State of being* is about cultivating our hearts to align with Jesus so that our expression of being is genuine. *State of doing* generates lists and then artificially goes through the motions. The Pharisees were more concerned with *doing* than they were with *being*, which led to a legalistic outlook. Groups that focus on *being* will never have to worry about their expressions of *doing*.

- *Organic over ordered.* Organic groups don't need to be told how to participate in each other's lives; they do it naturally and spontaneously. The natural relationships that form within groups cause people to pick up a phone and make last-minute plans. Whether catching a movie on impulse, meeting up for an impromptu dinner, popping in at the spur of the moment, or making unplanned trips to the grocery store together—organic groups see beyond their regularly scheduled meetings. They do so because they are naturally going through everyday life with the others in the group. They are always mindful of ways to be together and to enjoy life together.

• *Unity over uniformity.* Groups enjoy unity when they value diversity. Uniformity suggests that each person needs to meet a predetermined criterion of sameness. Unity values the unique contribution of distinctive personalities and dissimilar interests. Unity says, "If it wasn't for this group, I would never have associated with the others in this community." Unity seeks to experience a multicolored display of communal life, whereas uniformity seeks refuge in the monochromatic dysfunction of monotony.

The difference between leading a church and leading a movement is that the latter empowers followers of Jesus to shift from doing programs together to doing life together. This community experience forms over a series of moments—immediate, fleeting, and ephemeral. Yet in the space of these moments, something happens that transforms the human spirit in an unforgettable way. This transition into doing life together sets the backdrop for a great awakening and for the revelation of the incarnate Son of God. The curtain now begins to be pulled back on the reinventing of our name and the manifestation of the divine. Here's a hint: When you sense the boundaries of doing life together stretching you, that's the curtain beginning to be pulled. Embrace it!

11

dead men walking

Reinventing Our Name

Several years ago, I boarded a plane for the epicenter of devastation left over from Croatia's War of Independence. In 1991, Croatia declared its independence by holding the first democratic elections in the country, which led to a long and bloody war with local Serbs, who opposed independence.

The faces of the people revealed the horror of widespread killing, mass rape, ethnic cleansing, and torture. After driving several hours through bleak urban ghettos, our group—eight sheltered Americans—arrived at a small town on the outskirts of the capital. Escorted by United Nations troops, we crossed through barricades and checkpoints, walking the dismal corridors of disheveled streets. Everywhere we looked were the remains of charred buildings. We had been invited under the assurance of a cease-fire, but it was only a flimsy accord. Obviously the ones responsible for the gunfire and mortars exploding in the distance hadn't gotten the memo.

We entered a home and were greeted by a benevolent Croat family. Their friendly faces and hospitality were overwhelming. A quick tour revealed the frightful damage inflicted by Serbian shells. Walls were riddled with bullet holes. Their oven was still in use, despite the gaping hole that resulted from an explosive projectile. Their generosity astounded us as they insisted we sleep in their beds while their entire family of six slept on the cold, hard living room floor.

That evening, as I peered into their living room, I saw Jesus Christ. (Interesting, isn't it, how the living room is used again and again to reveal the presence of Jesus?) He didn't appear the way I had imagined him. He wasn't wearing a white toga with a purple sash, like you see in all the religious paraphernalia. He wasn't sporting sandals, a neatly groomed beard, or a flowing mane. I didn't recognize him at first, maybe because I was preoccupied with my own well-being—or maybe because my vision was restricted at first to seeing only what we were there to do. After all, we were the missionaries, there to introduce them to Jesus Christ. Yet I am certain it was him. Majestically he revealed himself through a loving Christian family as they slept.

For five days we lived with this family. We ate together, ministered together, prayed together, and worshiped together—and I continued to see Jesus through them. I will never forget the day I was told that the food they were providing for our few evening meals had cost them the equivalent of a month's worth of groceries. Every bite we took was a morsel of selflessness.

I struggled to make sense of it, constantly returning to the questions of *how* and *why*. In the midst of all the misery they had experienced, how and why could they exude such awe-inspiring character? The shock wave of their Jesus-ness sent tremors through my scandalized Christianity. They understood better than I did what it meant to embody the persona of Jesus Christ.

Icons of Influence

It's time we redeem the label put on by those of us who follow Jesus. Let's reclaim what *Christian* stands for. It is our heritage, our legacy, our trademark.

Merging our faith into real life will entail the resolve to help people embrace the magnitude of what it means to be a Christian—a disciple, a follower of Jesus. Jesus envisioned great things for his followers. All we have to do is believe, as Luke reminds us in his account of Paul and Silas and the jailer:

> [The jailer] brought [Paul and Silas] out and asked, "Sirs, what must I do to be saved?"
>
> They replied, "Believe in the Lord Jesus, and you will be saved—you and your household."
>
> ACTS 16:30–31

The radical life change of being conformed to the image of the Son of Man is about *becoming*. Becoming involves walking the ancient path of discipleship. It's an elemental part of our identity. I'm not talking about walking into a job interview and saying, "Hi, my name is Susan, and I am a disciple of Jesus Christ"; I'm talking about the correlation between what we believe and how we live our lives.

A disciple is someone who becomes an imitator of his or her respected tutor. At the epicenter of discipleship is the person whom the follower seeks to imitate—an icon, of sorts. A national icon is someone who, by the mere mention of their name, reminds people of their homeland. They are representatives of their nation to the rest of the world. People such as Michael Jordan, Jimi Hendrix, Marilyn Monroe, and Bruce Lee are recognized based on their celebrity status within a specific society. Icons serve as an inspiration of what people can become. The whole success of *American Idol* is based on the power of icon; the show fuels the premise that anybody can become a superstar like Kelly Clarkson, Carrie Underwood, or David Cook.

Whether we admit it or not, we are influenced by the icons of our world. Every culture embraces some form of icons — whether political, pop, religious, or corporate. These icons tend to inspire and even define us. The crux of our becoming like Jesus is our choosing him to be our icon. Faith in real life is about making Jesus the focal point. The writer of Hebrews alluded to this principle:

> Let us run with perseverance the race marked out for us, fixing our eyes on Jesus, the pioneer and perfecter of faith. For the joy set before him he endured the cross, scorning its shame, and sat down at the right hand of the throne of God. Consider him who endured such opposition from sinners, so that you will not grow weary and lose heart.
>
> HEBREWS 12:1–3

Infrastructures of Influence

Have you ever wondered why Jesus didn't write anything in the Bible? He spoke and others recorded what he said, but he could have communicated everything he wanted by jotting down a thesis or a composition. Instead, he chose to spend his time investing in a handful of individuals so they could write the story. His legacy was bound up in the ragged band of misfits who would end up accomplishing great things. As Jesus taught his disciples, "Very truly I tell you, all who have faith in me will do the works I have been doing, and they will do even greater things than these, because I am going to the Father" (John 14:12).

Jesus not only demonstrated community; he created an infrastructure of influence. He was the cause of his own effect. Deep inside, all of us long to be with people who will validate us, encourage us, and care for us. Beyond these essentials, togetherness also provokes, stretches, and stimulates us to do things we could never accomplish alone. In the community of Jesus' disciples, we see individuals who joined together in a cause greater than themselves. To their surprise, they discover that their own needs were met as they served each other.

Community provides the ultimate infrastructure of influence, propelling us into action and arousing us to become activists who influence the world around us. Community captures the organic expression of the church mobilized. God is unleashing something powerful in our groups of eight to twelve people who meet regularly in living rooms to live out his purpose of community. They are reclaiming the ancient definition of what it means to be a disciple, a follower, a Christian. Today's movement is not only about belonging; it's about becoming spiritually healthy. And that's the kind of DNA we are striving for in our missional groups.

Small groups are more than just a place to connect. The primary motive behind our small groups is the aspiration to create an infrastructure of influence for cause and effect. The difference between leading a church and leading a movement is the ability to strategically place people within this infrastructure of relational influence.

The writer of Hebrews captures this idea: "Let us consider how we may spur one another on toward love and good deeds, not giving up meeting together, as some are in the habit of doing, but encouraging one another — and all the more as you see the Day approaching" (Hebrews 10:24 – 25).

Whenever I read this passage, I picture the infamous scene in the movie *A Christmas Story*. Ralphie's friends Flick and Schwartz argue over whether a person's tongue will stick to a frozen flagpole. Schwartz ultimately issues Flick a "triple dog dare," and Flick's tongue gets stuck to the pole, much to their terror. Much like a triple dog dare, the word *spur* means to "to provoke" or "to stimulate." When left in isolation, we seldom take the risks that a group might encourage us to take. The writer to the Hebrews exhorted first-century Christians to not give up meeting together in community because it offered the best opportunity to stimulate one another.

Recently I heard an amazing story in one of our staff meetings. We offer a small group experience we call LinC (Living in Community). The goal of LinC is to help people discover what missional community is all about. It's offered to all of our new guests as a way of helping them discover from the beginning what we are all about and where we want people to grow in their relationship with Jesus. The aim of LinC is to spur people to engage in something they would never do on their own.

The LinC group heard about a new church plant that was starting up in our neighborhood. During a brainstorming session, someone came up with the idea of attending the church plant's next service in order to support them and pray with them. She invited others to join her, and another person immediately objected that he was hesitant to pray out loud, particularly in front of strangers. But that evening, the group met with the leadership team of the new church plant—and who do you think was the first person to pray aloud? Yes, it was the gentleman who, just a few hours earlier, was convinced he could never do such a thing. Influence is all about relationship. When people belong to a group of friends who motivate and encourage each other, they are stretched to do things they would never have done on their own. It causes them to set aside personal fear in order to step out.

The Man of Influence

Paul had an ambitious desire to see the followers of Jesus experience life change within the context of community:

> So Christ himself gave the apostles, the prophets, the evangelists, the pastors and teachers, to equip his people for works of service, so that the body of Christ may be built up until we all reach unity in the faith and in the knowledge of the Son of God and become mature, attaining to the whole measure of the fullness of Christ.
>
> EPHESIANS 4:11 – 13

Paul nailed it in this passage. He made a brilliant correlation between "attaining to the *whole* measure of the fullness of Christ" and the body of Christ being built up. Essentially Paul was talking about a second incarnation of Christ.

A very confused disciple named Philip once asked Jesus to show him the Father. Jesus responded in what sounded like a tone of frustration: "Don't you know me, Philip, even after I have been among you such a long time? Anyone who has seen me has seen the Father. How can you say, 'Show us the Father'?" (John 14:9).

Jesus Christ embodied the fullness or wholeness of God. Here is how the writer of Hebrews described this majestic representation:

> In the past God spoke to our ancestors through the prophets at many times and in various ways, but in these last days he has spoken to us by his Son, whom he appointed heir of all things, and through whom also he made the universe. The

Son is the radiance of God's glory and the exact representation of his being, sustaining all things by his powerful word.

HEBREWS 1:1–3

Through the Word becoming flesh, we are given a marvelous
insight into who God is. We do not roam the earth in search of
an unknown god hiding beneath a shroud of obscurity. God has
revealed himself brilliantly in the person of his Son, Jesus Christ.

The Church of Influence

Jesus continues to personify or expose himself in "the whole
measure," the "fullness," through his body, the church. Paul
had pointed this out earlier in Ephesians: "And God placed all
things under [Christ's] feet and appointed him to be head over
everything for the church, which is his body, the fullness of him
who fills everything in every way" (Ephesians 1:22–23).

How bizarre! When I think of the church, I don't automatically think, "Hey, there goes the fullness of Christ." Usually I
think, "Hey, there goes a bunch of messed-up people."

Paul, though, is quick to acknowledge key leadership roles
within the body: apostles, prophets, evangelists, and pastors and
teachers. He points out that their function is to "equip [God's]
people for works of service" (Ephesians 4:12). The Greek word
for "service" here is *diakonia*; it conveys the idea of mutual
ministry shared by members of the community of faith. It is
a communal term that implies a coming alongside one another
as we serve each other in every area of our lives—physically,
emotionally, socially, and spiritually. The result of these selfless
acts of service is that "the body of Christ may be built up."

The Greek word translated "built up" is *oikodomē*; the same
word is translated "edification" in Romans 14:19. It suggests the

promotion of another person's spiritual growth. The point is that spiritual gifts and the service they render were designed for one purpose, namely, edification. Joining gifting and service together in the context of community can ignite explosive growth in the lives of believers.

Paul then reveals that the process of building each other up leads to "unity in the faith and in the knowledge of the Son of God" (Ephesians 4:13). This results in believers becoming "mature." The Greek word translated "mature" is *teleios*, which captures the idea of completion. The signpost of Christian maturity is not in our knowledge of the Bible or in the regularity of our tithing. It's not in our church attendance; it's not even in our status as church leaders. It's only discovered in the Christlike rendering that humbly manifests itself in every dimension of our being.

How does a group measure its progress toward Christlikeness? As intelligent human beings, we are always trying to measure our spirituality. It's our way of knowing and controlling the potential outcome. We approach our spiritual formation as though it were a well-executed football play, complete with carefully thought-out strategies and clear ways of measuring how far we've come and how far we still have to go.

Let me share a word of caution: Throughout the history of the church, its leaders have constantly tried to manufacture new systems and programs to aid in spiritual formation. Becoming like Christ is not about working harder to mimic his DNA; it's not something we can chart on a diagram. Becoming like Christ begins with knowing and loving him in a personal relationship. Consider the warning of Jesus to the church in Ephesus:

> To the angel of the church in Ephesus write:
>   These are the words of him who holds the seven stars in his right hand and walks among the seven golden

lampstands: I know your deeds, your hard work and your perseverance. I know that you cannot tolerate wicked people, that you have tested those who claim to be apostles but are not, and have found them false. You have persevered and have endured hardships for my name, and have not grown weary.

Yet I hold this against you: You have forsaken the love you had at first. Consider how far you have fallen! Repent and do the things you did at first. If you do not repent, I will come to you and remove your lampstand from its place.

REVELATION 2:1–5

Those are harsh words. Ironically, in the Ephesian believers' well-intentioned efforts to know Christ and make him known, they had actually forsaken the love they had at first. But you wouldn't have known they had left their first love by looking at their activity. Outwardly, they were doing great! Compare this to Jesus' words to the church at Sardis:

These are the words of him who holds the seven spirits of God and the seven stars. I know your deeds; you have a reputation of being alive, but you are dead. Wake up! Strengthen what remains and is about to die, for I have found your deeds unfinished in the sight of my God.

REVELATION 3:1–2

After surveying their wonderful deeds, which fueled the reputation that they were one happening church, Jesus gave them a painful reality check: "You're dead. Wake up!" This was a church that was doing all the right things for God, yet they were dead spiritually. Their deeds were found incomplete because they defined success in terms of those deeds instead of the fullness of Christ. Churches under human leadership can accomplish some incredible things, but these accomplishments don't automatically indicate the presence of Christ.

We are indwelt by the same Holy Spirit who indwelt and shaped the first believers. Paul explained that the Holy Spirit is the one who shapes our understanding of Christ through his revelation. Missional community makes room for the Holy Spirit to breathe the life of Christ into everyone. Notice how Paul, as he writes to the Corinthians, reminds them that they become complete through the transformation into the likeness of Christ. He emphasizes that the Spirit is the transforming agent: "We all, who with unveiled faces contemplate the Lord's glory, are being transformed into his image with ever-increasing glory, which comes from the Lord, who is the Spirit" (2 Corinthians 3:18).

Knowing that we are becoming more complete in the expressed fullness of Christ is evidenced by the fruit of the Spirit: love, joy, peace, patience, kindness, goodness, faithfulness, gentleness, and self-control (Galatians 5:22–23).

A significant part of the transformation process is the restructuring of how we think. Missional community is about shared experiences that challenge our understanding of what it means to follow Christ: "Do not conform to the pattern of this world, but be transformed by the renewing of your mind" (Romans 12:2).

The renewal of the mind is a radical shift in perception, resulting in everything being viewed differently. The point is that believers begin to perceive what was previously unfathomable because they have the very Spirit of Christ in them. The renewal of the mind is a call for community thinking and discernment that is not patterned after this world. Learning in our modernistic world is all about individual intelligence; learning in a postmodern world is a shared experience. Postmodern knowledge relies on a social process that holistically involves the emotions, experience, and the intellect.

Paul did not suggest merely an individual renewal of mind, but a united, communal renewal of mind: "I appeal to you, brothers and sisters, in the name of our Lord Jesus Christ, that all of you agree with one another in what you say and that there be no divisions among you, but that you be perfectly united in mind and thought" (1 Corinthians 1:10).

This communal renewal of the mind represents a countercultural outlook on life. Missional community depends on the Spirit to bring the values of Christ to the forefront of our minds. These shared values form a common cause. Missional community is about provoking and stimulating one another to embrace and express these shared values.

Extreme Faith

Becoming a follower of Jesus is not something done on a whim or without considerable cost. When Jesus called his first followers, he assured them that this journey would be about formation and becoming. He promised he would make them into something:

> As Jesus was walking beside the Sea of Galilee, he saw two brothers, Simon called Peter and his brother Andrew. They were casting a net into the lake, for they were fishermen. "Come, follow me," Jesus said, "and I will send you out to fish for people." At once they left their nets and followed him.
>
> MATTHEW 4:18–20

Jesus also told his disciples that to follow him would cost them something: "Whoever wants to be my disciple must deny themselves and take up their cross and follow me" (Matthew 16:24).

Put yourselves in the sandals of those young, unassuming men. One afternoon, Jesus led them on an enterprising excursion to Caesarea Philippi. In this exceptional moment, Jesus decided to issue a pop quiz: "Who do people say the Son of Man is?" After a few of them responded by repeating other people's theories, Peter confessed, "You are the Messiah, the Son of the living God" (Matthew 16:16). Then Jesus began to tell them about his destiny: death.

I love Peter's response. He thought Jesus had flipped out of his mind. Peter pulled him aside and whispered, "This shall never happen to you!" (Matthew 16:22). Jesus answered Peter with a stern command, telling him that he was under the influence of Satan and that he had better not get in the way of Jesus' divine calling. In essence, Jesus told his disciples (and us), "If you want to follow me, death to self is the prerequisite, and you are going to have to carry your own cross to the grave." I wonder if some of them thought, "Yeah right, I'm outta here."

These days, we like to think of "taking up your cross" as a metaphor. But living under Roman rule in a land that was littered with crucifixions, every disciple must have known that they were dead men walking. For them, following Jesus meant suicide. Jesus didn't mince words about that either: "Whoever finds their life will lose it, and whoever loses their life for my sake will find it" (Matthew 10:39). Even today, following Jesus is a sort of suicide. It will cost us something—but the payoff is so worth it.

Jesus was not inviting his disciples to join a Bible study so they could improve their scriptural dexterity. He wasn't inviting them into a small clique of friends so they could feel connected. He wasn't inviting them into a support group so their insecurities and wounds could be caressed. He wasn't inviting them into a prayer group so they could have all of their prayers and petitions answered.

His invitation was to partake of a life defined by risk and reward. After all, the apostle Paul wrote, "To live is Christ and to die is gain" (Philippians 1:21). It was one long, adventurous group outing through treacherous lands where the blind received sight, the hungry were miraculously fed, devils were expelled, people walked on water, the dead came back to life, fish sank boats, and thousands were liberated from the tyranny of religious oppression.

Jesus was leading a small group who always had something to write home about—and never a second thought of splitting the group up (with the exception of Judas). They were united in their revolutionary cause. Jesus led them in an audacious goal of transforming the world.

If today's followers of Jesus would embrace the dangerous and thrilling pursuit of living in missional community as Jesus did, we would finally wake up from our sleepy spirituality.

I understand that this kind of living is more an anomaly than it is the norm. As followers of Jesus, though, it's our responsibility to cultivate this type of radical community—one that is lived in the cubicles of our offices, the cul-de-sacs of our neighborhoods, and the ghettos of our cities.

This is not about outward appearance. That's piety. It's about a posture of expectancy—the anticipation that we will hear the voice of the Spirit and be willing to respond. We cultivate it by living it ourselves and inviting others to participate with us. Church leaders often manipulate artificial responses through coercion and superficial programming. But living it, breathing it, and celebrating it will do more to empower people than anything else we may do.

A year ago, Grace Chapel changed the way we do leadership training. Instead of tedious informational meetings, we
now organize leader field trips throughout the year. These trips
are designed to give us opportunities to live out the values of
missional community. Most leaders would rather engage holistically than get another intellectual brain dump. We have discovered that through this method of equipping, leaders become
refreshed and prepared to guide others in the missional journey.

Most Christians have not had the opportunity to experience this type of radical community. As G. K. Chesterton
once wrote, "The Christian ideal has not been tried and found
wanting. It has been found difficult; and left untried."[19] Faith
in real life means helping people embrace the radical process
of "attaining to the whole measure of the fullness of Christ"
(Ephesians 4:13). As Paul wrote to the believers in Philippi,

> Not that I have already obtained all this, or have already
> arrived at my goal, but I press on to take hold of that for
> which Christ Jesus took hold of me. Brothers and sisters, I
> do not consider myself yet to have taken hold of it. But one
> thing I do: Forgetting what is behind and straining toward
> what is ahead, I press on toward the goal to win the prize
> for which God has called me heavenward in Christ Jesus.
>
> PHILIPPIANS 3:12–14

Final Words for the Journey

This is the part where I'm supposed to issue a final charge—
to say something that will inspire you to be more intentional,
more inspired, or more courageous in living out this expression
of faith. The ideas I've shared are not meant to be a foolproof,
patented plan with a guarantee of instant success or miraculous

results. They are ordinary words soaked in sweat, blood, and failures.

Even as I write these final thoughts, I face a whole set of new obstacles as I seek to discover what God has in mind for his church. I don't believe he ever intended us to find easy formulas; doing so would be boring! Instead, I think he keeps us on the front edge of mystery and wonder—desperately dependent on his hand to guide and move us. And maybe, just maybe, his hand will shake us enough to provoke a response of abandonment—leaving the past behind in order to embrace the future that he has in store for those who follow him in the great adventure of his redemptive plan.

I pray that God will give each of us the courage and inspiration to embark on the journey of becoming the fullness of Christ in our communities of faith in real life.

P.S. The next time you see a Chihuahua, say hello for me!

reading group guide

The following questions are designed to help you think through the content of this book as it relates to your own life and ministry. There are two sets of questions for each chapter, one set directed to ministry leaders and the second to followers. It is worth looking through both sets of questions, regardless of your current role in ministry. A Christlike leader is first and foremost a follower, and so both sets of questions are applicable. For those who do not consider themselves to be in a leadership role, you can benefit from considering the leader questions by thinking about how you would answer them if you were leading a ministry or by putting yourself in the shoes of a leader you know. For each chapter, keep in mind three overarching questions:

1. What story or idea stood out to you the most, and why?
2. What do you agree with, and why?
3. What do you disagree with, and why?

Part 1: the new church

1: the church and the chihuahua club

Further Reflection for Leaders

1. In your own words, what is a leader?

2. What experiences have been used by God to shape you to lead others?

3. Have you ever felt the tension between wanting to run from a ministry where you've made a commitment to stay? What was the end result of the situation?

4. At the end of the chapter, success was defined and measured by life change. How do you measure success in your church/ministry?

Further Reflection for Followers

1. How did you view the church growing up? Is your view of the church any different today, and if so, what changed?

2. What image best illustrates for you what the church is supposed to be?

3. In which area do you think the church needs to experience the most change?

4. In what ways do we do our church a disservice when we take the easy way out and run from issues when things get messy and uncomfortable?

2: process this

Further Reflection for Leaders

1. What is your approach (or your church's approach) to discipleship?

2. What are five advantages and five disadvantages of focusing on discipleship programs instead of a process tailor-made to each individual?

3. In evangelism and discipleship we move people "from community to community" (p. 43). Give an example from your own life or ministry.

4. The park, coffee shop, and living room metaphors illustrate the process of deepening relational intimacy. What intentional method do you use to encourage relational depth in your church body?

Further Reflection for Followers

1. How does viewing church as a one-day event instead of a daily process hinder our spiritual growth?

2. Discipleship is a personal journey, and we are ultimately responsible for our own growth, but in what ways is the discipleship journey a community process?

3. The park, coffee shop, and living room metaphors illustrate the process of deepening relational intimacy. Think of one of your close friends and describe the process that caused a stranger to become a close friend.

4. How can you be more intentional about developing deeper ties with the people in your church?

3: mad dogs and gladiators

Further Reflection for Leaders

1. Are you aligned to the vision of God, or are you aligning God to your vision? How do you know?

2. What is your church's mission and purpose? Are all the ministries aligned to that purpose?

3. How essential to a sustainable mission are "raising up" and "reaching out"? What would happen if you only focused on one?

4. "The purpose of the church is to respond to God's revelation" (p. 55). In what ways is church a response to God's revelation? What is one thing your ministry is doing that may be stifling people's response?

5. This chapter lists a number of cultural differences that formed in the transition from the modern period to the postmodern. Which one resonates with you the most? Take one of the items from the list and give an example of how you can leverage it to enhance the experience of community

Further Reflection for Followers

1. Change is inevitable, and so ministry leaders continually face the stress of managing change. What can you do to support and affirm your leaders as they implement necessary changes?

2. What is your church's purpose, mission, and vision? (If you don't know, how can you find out?)

3. "The purpose of the church is to respond to God's revelation" (p. 55). What was the most recent step you took to respond to something you have learned in your faith journey?

4. As you think about the things you are passionate about, skilled in, and gifted in, list a few ideas of how you can bring your unique contribution to your church's mission?

Part 2: **the park**

4: hermaphrodites and other lovable people

Further Reflection for Leaders

1. Do you know your community's needs, or are you making assumptions?

2. Where are some of the places you can go to find this information? Who in your church has connections to these hubs so that you can invite them to help establish relationships?

3. What are your church's key resources (personal and practical) to offer your community?

4. Which of the 3Cs (contact, consistency, connection; p. 97) do you need to put more effort into as you try to connect with natural hubs of influence?

Further Reflection for Followers

1. In your opinion, what makes a church relevant?

2. How do you feel about the description of the church as "the heart of the city"?

3. In what ways is your church actively changing culture?

4. What connections of influence do you have with the key hubs in your community, and how can you make them available to your church to enhance their presence to the community?

5. Are you willing to engage in ministries that make you uncomfortable in order to support your church leaders as they model Christ to your community?

5: eggsactly wrong

Further Reflection for Leaders

1. What emotions do you experience when you think about "marketing the church"? If someone from outside your church took a look at how you invest your time, energy, and money, what conclusion would they draw about the character of Christ?

2. What can you do to expose people in your ministry to the pain and suffering in your community?

3. Are you (or is your church) invested in fighting any of the social justice issues listed at the end of the chapter (p. 120)? What can you do to increase awareness in your body?

4. What local ministries and parachurch organizations are addressing the issues in your community? What are the advantages and disadvantages to partnering with these organizations in addressing your community's needs?

Further Reflection for Followers

1. When we become disciples of Christ our lives are living examples of Christ to the world. If someone was to follow you around and observe your life, what conclusions would they draw about who Christ is?

2. When was the last time you witnessed or experienced a radical act of kindness? How did it affect you?

3. Are you (or is your church) passionate about any of the social justice issues listed at the end of the chapter (p. 120)?

4. Churches are often involved in doing amazing work that goes unnoticed. What can you do to help market the character of Christ that is demonstrated through your church?

6: the wounded beast

Further Reflection for Leaders

1. Imagine that the church has no history and Jesus Christ has personally given you the assignment to go and make disciples. With no church philosophy, models, or paradigms to rely on, how would you carry out this task? In what ways does your answer differ from your current expression of church?

2. What is the purpose of your Sunday gathering? Do you expect God to show up? Do you leave room for the Holy Spirit to move?

3. Of the elements of a church service listed in this chapter, which ones are strengths for your church and which are areas for improvement? Are there any elements left out that you would include on your list?

4. When was the last time you personally encountered God at church?

Further Reflection for Followers

1. Imagine that the church has no history and Jesus Christ has personally given you the assignment to go and make disciples. With no church philosophy, models, or paradigms to rely on, how would you carry out this task?

2. What criteria were significant in choosing to attend your church?

3. Describe *passionate worship.*

4. Do you go to church expecting God to show up?

5. When was the last time you had a personal encounter with God at church?

Part 3: **the coffee shop**

7: a rabbi, a muzungu, and the twilight zone

Further Reflection for Leaders

1. In your ministry do you have an intentional process for moving people into deeper levels of relationship?

2. What are your church's "coffee shop" environments?

3. What are the predominant issues that keep people from being fully engaged in your church community?

4. As you review the relational hurdles listed in this chapter, which are most prevalent in your church/ministry?

5. Looking at this same list, which ones do you personally struggle with?

Further Reflection for Followers

1. Thinking through the "coffee shop" metaphor, what would you list as your church's "coffee shop" environments?

2. What level of relational connection do you normally experience at your regular hangout spot? Do you have a similar degree of relationship in any aspect of church life?

3. What does it look like to be fully involved in the life of your church community?

4. As you review the relational hurdles listed in the chapter, which ones keep you from being fully invested in your church community? Do you experience any hurdles that aren't listed?

8: polyester suits notwithstanding

Further Reflection for Leaders

1. Diagram your process for getting people plugged in to church. Where are the leaps that can cause people to disengage? How can you close this gap?

2. How important is follow-up in helping people invest in community?

3. This chapter lists a number of possible relational spaces that provide opportunities to connect (pp. 166–68). Of the ones listed, which ones do you offer? How have you seen these impact people?

4. How does exposing your church to real-life stories of life change in community affect people's view of the value of intimate community?

5. How does *really* listening build trust and create the right to be heard?

Further Reflection for Followers

1. What holds you back from opening up to other people?

2. Has your excitement ever fizzled out because no one followed up with you?

3. This chapter lists a number of possible relational spaces that provide opportunities to connect (pp. 166–68). Which of these are most appealing to you? Do any of your church's ministries fall into these categories?

4. What can church leaders do to encourage you to get more involved in the lives of the people at your church?

Part 4: the living room

9: fire in the house

Further Reflection for Leaders

1. How important is relational depth to life change?

2. How can you utilize relational depth to increase your level of influence with those you lead?

3. Does the way you express yourself in ministry show that you value all the parts of the body of Christ, or does it look more like you're trying to create clones?

4. Often the more upfront gifts get the most accolades. How do you celebrate and validate the "background" gifts?

5. "Compartmentalizing is hazardous to our spiritual health" (p. 179). How do you balance leaving your work at church and not compartmentalizing your faith?

Further Reflection for Followers

1. Using the example of a blossoming romantic relationship, describe the natural process of deepening a relationship. What environments mark each stage of the relationship?

2. How does your comfort level differ between being in a

friend's home and being in stranger's home? How does it affect your likelihood of sharing something intimate?

3. "Compartmentalizing is hazardous to our spiritual health" (p. 179). How does compartmentalizing hinder a full life in Christ?

4. Why is intimate community so hard? How can the lessons learned from recapturing the essence of community help the longevity of marriages and the stability of families?

5. When you share your story, what parts do you hold back?

chapter 10: turtles with their necks out

Further Reflection for Leaders

1. How important is our response to someone's vulnerability in fostering a safe environment? What happens when someone is shot down?

2. Look at the description of a place of unconditional love (p. 194). What aspect of this is your church fostering, and what needs more work?

3. The chapter ends with a list of changes that need to be made in order to return to a deeper expression of community. Which traits need the most work in your church/ministry? How can you use these to go deeper?

4. How does valuing your diversity bring about unity? What do you do to encourage diversity?

Further Reflection for Followers

1. How do you feel about the kind of community described on page 198? Which item is most appealing to you?

2. What do people hear when you talk about your church (Love? Hate? Anger? Bitterness? Excitement?), and how does it affect how outsiders perceive the church?

3. Have you experienced belonging? What did it look like to belong? What got you there, or what stopped you?

4. What do you think of the statement "you get out of community what you put into it"?

chapter 11: dead men walking

Further Reflection for Leaders

1. Does it bother you that the term *Christian* has become so negative to people?

2. Do the things you promote and the way you live correlate?

3. Would people describe you as uplifting or critical? How do these qualities affect your influence over someone?

4. As you look at the influential people in your body, how can developing a relationship with them increase your level of influence over your body?

5. What is the danger of trying to package the processes of relational and spiritual growth in simple formulas?

Further Reflection for Followers

1. Does it bother you that the term *Christian* has become so negative to people? Does your life show Christ in a positive or a negative light?

2. Jesus said that people would know we are his disciples by our love for one another (John 13:35). Do your relationships with and attitude toward people in your church model a loving

community that draws people, or does it push them away from church?

3. In what ways do our needs get met as we serve others?

4. Are you willing to pay the price of following Christ? What costs have you experienced so far?

acknowledgments

For a young boy once considered illiterate, this work was made possible by those who had the courage to believe in me and who accompanied me on the journey.

Dad—because you modeled it
Mom—because you nurtured it
Bernadette—because you stand with me in it
Carol—because you exude it
Mark—because you sharpen me in it
Jason—because you encourage me in it
Brad—because you affirm me in it
Mikiah and Jadon—because you are the legacy of it
James—because you gave me the platform for it
Dennis and Nikki—because you bring depth to it
Angela—because you advocated it
The LifeWay Community—because you inspired it
Toni and Serena—because you risked it
CLG—because you live it
GC staff—because you shape it
GC elders—because you fueled it
GC community—because you respond to it
Life Group leaders—because you are the catalyst for it

notes

1. Erwin McManus, *Soul Cravings* (Nashville: Nelson, 2006), 4.
2. Mark Driscoll, *The Radical Reformission* (Grand Rapids: Zondervan, 2004), 78.
3. Reggie McNeal, *The Present Future* (San Francisco: Jossey-Bass, 2003), 15.
4. Michael Frost and Alan Hirsch, *The Shaping of Things to Come* (Peabody, Mass.: Hendrickson, 2003), 15–16.
5. Stanley J. Grenz, *A Primer on Postmodernism* (Grand Rapids: Eerdmans, 1996), 14.
6. Thomas S. Rainer and Eric Geiger, *Simple Church* (Nashville: B&H Publishing, 2006), 125.
7. Edward B. Tylor, *Primitive Culture* (London: Murray, 1871), 1.
8. "Thriller," written and composed by Rod Temperton (1983); performed by Michael Jackson.
9. Tim Keller, "Ministry in the New Global Culture of Major City Centers (Part IV)," *http://www.redeemer2.com/themovement/issues/2006/spring/ministry_in_globalculture_IV.html*.
10. David Kinnaman and Gabe Lyons, *UnChristian* (Grand Rapids: Baker, 2007), 18.
11. Tim Stafford, "Servant Evangelism," *Christianity Today* 52 (November 2008): 43.
12. Brian McLaren, *The Church on the Other Side* (3d ed.; Grand Rapids: Zondervan, 2006), 88.
13. Jim Wallis, *The Great Awakening* (New York: HarperOne, 2008), 219.

14. Erwin McManus, *An Unstoppable Force* (Loveland, Colo.: Group, 2001), 117–18.

15. Bill Donahue and Russ Robinson, *Building a Church of Small Groups* (Grand Rapids: Zondervan, 2001), 22.

16. Brian McLaren, *The Story We Find Ourselves In* (San Francisco: Jossey-Bass, 2003), 121.

17. Joseph H. Mayfield and Ralph Earle, *John–Acts* (Beacon Bible Commentary; Kansas City: Beacon Hill, 1965), 161.

18. Julie Gorman, *Community That Is Christian* (Wheaton, Ill.: Victor, 1993), 48.

19. G. K. Chesterton, *What's Wrong with the World* (London: Cassell, 1910), 39.

Share Your Thoughts

With the Author: Your comments will be forwarded to the author when you send them to *zauthor@zondervan.com*.

With Zondervan: Submit your review of this book by writing to *zreview@zondervan.com*.

Free Online Resources at
www.zondervan.com

Zondervan AuthorTracker: Be notified whenever your favorite authors publish new books, go on tour, or post an update about what's happening in their lives at www.zondervan.com/authortracker.

Daily Bible Verses and Devotions: Enrich your life with daily Bible verses or devotions that help you start every morning focused on God. Visit www.zondervan.com/newsletters.

Free Email Publications: Sign up for newsletters on Christian living, academic resources, church ministry, fiction, children's resources, and more. Visit www.zondervan.com/newsletters.

Zondervan Bible Search: Find and compare Bible passages in a variety of translations at www.zondervanbiblesearch.com.

Other Benefits: Register yourself to receive online benefits like coupons and special offers, or to participate in research.

ZONDERVAN®

ZONDERVAN.com/
AUTHORTRACKER
follow your favorite authors